The Art of
STRIKING

—

The Art of
STRIKING

PRINCIPLES & TECHNIQUES

MARC TEDESCHI

Weatherhill

FIRST EDITION, 2002
First Printing

Book and cover design: Marc Tedeschi
Photography: Shelley Firth, Frank Deras
Creative consultant: Michele Wetherbee
Editorial supervision: Ray Furse, Thomas Tedeschi
Printing and binding: Oceanic Graphic Printing
and C&C Offset Printing in China
Typeset in Helvetica Neue, Univers, Sabon,
Adobe Garamond, Weiss, and Times.

Library of Congress Cataloging-in-Publication Data
Tedeschi, Marc.
    The art of striking: principles & techniques /
    Marc Tedeschi. —1st ed.
        p. cm.
    Includes bibliographical references.
    ISBN 0-8348-0495-6
    1. Martial arts—Striking. I. Title
GV1102.7.S82 .T43 2002
793.8—dc21   2001045438

Notice of Liability

The information in this book is distributed without warranty and is only presented as a means of preserving a unique aspect of the heritage of the martial arts. All information and techniques are to be used at the reader's sole discretion. While every precaution has been taken in preparation of this book, neither the author nor publisher shall have any liability to any person or entity with respect to liability, loss, or damage caused or alleged to be caused directly or indirectly by the contents contained in this book or by the procedures or processes described herein. There is no guarantee that the techniques described or shown in this book will be safe or effective in any self-defense or medical situation, or otherwise. You may be injured if you apply or train in the techniques described in this book. Consult a physician regarding whether or not to attempt any technique described in this book. Specific self-defense responses illustrated in this book may not be justified in any particular situation in view of all of the circumstances or under the applicable federal, state, or local laws.

Trademarks:
Kuk Sool Won™ and Hwa Rang Do® are claimed as trademarks of their respective owners.

—

*For all those who
cultivate modesty, humility,
and the fierce courage
to constantly reinvent
their own destiny.*

—

CONTENTS

Editorial Notes
The information in this book is a
reorganized and expanded version
of material found in the author's
1136-page *Hapkido*, and employs
similar editorial conventions:
To avoid sexist grammar, *they*,
them, *their*, and *themselves*
are used in place of the singular
pronouns *he*, *she*, *him*, *her*,
his, *hers*, *himself*, and *herself*.
To avoid wordiness, articles may
be omitted, and abbreviations are
employed: (R) for right, (L) for left.

This book outlines the essential principles and techniques that define the art of striking in most martial arts. The technical differences between most martial styles are defined by the unique ways in which they use and combine skills. This is largely determined by philosophical ideas, as the techniques themselves are often very similar. The reasons for this are not difficult to grasp: since all martial techniques seek to capitalize on strengths and limitations of the human form, they by necessity come to similar conclusions and embody similar

OVERVIEW

technical principles. While these principles may be expressed differently in different styles, they usually reflect the same basic concepts. The techniques in this book come from Hapkido, a varied and practical martial art that shares historical and technical similarities with many other arts, such as Taekwondo, Jujutsu, Aikido, Karate, Kempo, Kung Fu, Kuk Sool Won, and Hwa Rang Do. It is hoped this book will enrich your practice, regardless of style, and help you to recognize your style's place within the larger culture of martial arts.

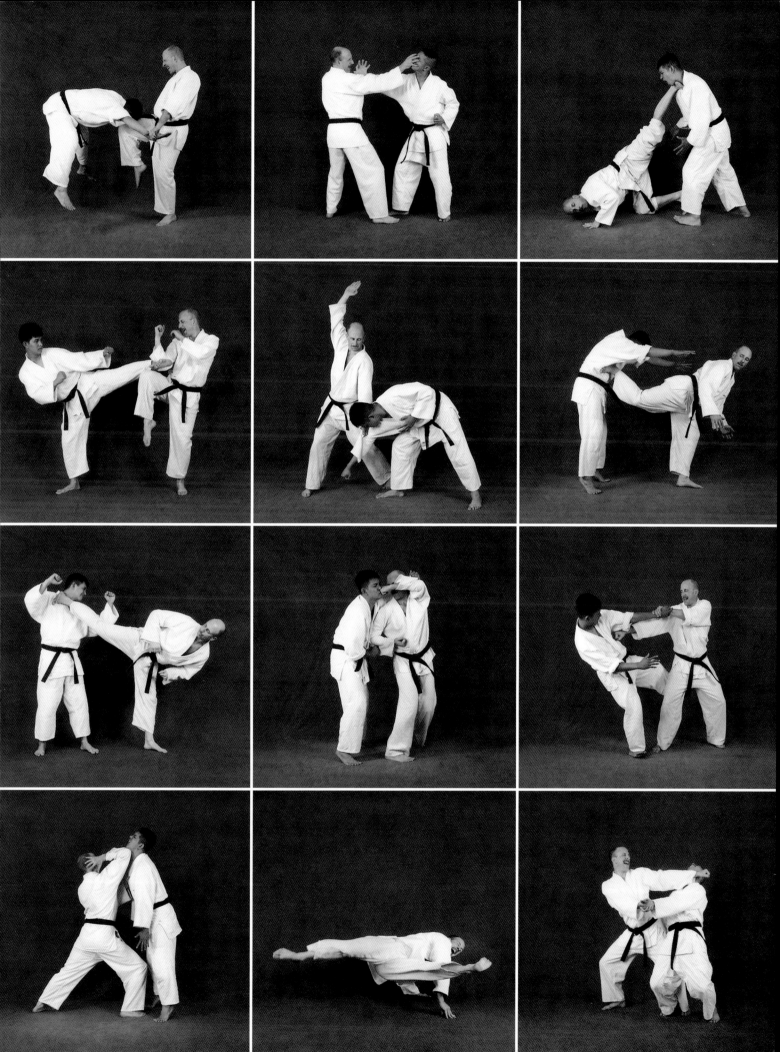

Introduction

The strike techniques of any martial art are defined by which body surfaces are used for hitting, how blows are delivered, what targets are struck, and the intended purpose of the strike (deter, cripple, kill). Blows are usually delivered to another person's body, but may also be used to strike an object such as a door, shield, obstacle, or weapon. In comprehensive self-defense arts, such as Hapkido, strikes are used for offensive or defensive purposes, from standing or ground positions.

In *hard styles* such as Karate, powerful penetrating strikes are delivered from strengthened and hardened body surfaces, to any part of the body. The objective is often to break bone or damage organs and tissue by striking vital or vulnerable areas. Blows are sometimes delivered by directly opposing an opponent's force. The entire body is usually committed to generating and supporting the strike's power.

In *soft styles,* less power is used, but the strike is directed to highly sensitive areas (nerves, tendons, pressure points, vital areas) to increase the strike's effectiveness. Blows are often delivered during a blending or joining movement in which the force of the strike joins with the attacker's force. This is very useful when facing an overpowering attacker, or when you wish to minimize potential damage to yourself (from striking), or to your opponent (from being struck). When compared to hard strikes, conditioning of hitting surfaces becomes less important, since force at impact is greatly reduced on the hitting surface.

Both methods of striking have advantages and disadvantages. Hard strikes require less accuracy than soft strikes, but you are more liable to damage your hitting surface unless it is well formed and conditioned. Hard strikes to soft targets are much safer and more effective. Soft strikes to highly sensitive targets are *very* effective as long as you are extremely accurate. This is not so easily accomplished on a moving target. Additionally, sensitivity at specific nerve points varies widely by individual. Some people may not react at all.

The material in this book will cover basic principles and skills, common strikes, combinations, and defenses against strikes and grabs—all of the categories that typically define the art of striking. Most of the techniques in this book are shown in the context of self-defense; however, sport-oriented martial arts will often embody similar principles. In eclectic arts, such as Hapkido, *striking* is never thought of as an isolated body of techniques, but rather as an integral part of a larger system embracing a range of martial skills (holds, throws, grappling, etc.). Those martial artists seeking an eclectic, comprehensive approach to self-defense, should obtain the author's 1136-page book, *Hapkido: Traditions, Philosophy, Technique.*

Types of Strikes

Martial strikes are executed using about 60 different body surfaces, involving hands, arms, feet, knees, legs, elbows, torso, and the head. Strikes may be used singularly, in continuous repetition, in combination with other strikes, or in combination with other techniques such as blocks, holds, and throws. This book documents over 160 basic strikes, which can be varied or combined in limitless ways based upon tactics and end use requirements. Strikes in this book are organized according to the part of the body used to deliver a blow. The basic categories are:

- Arm Strikes
- Leg Strikes
- Head and Body Strikes

Triple combination strike to multiple opponents

Strike Mechanics

Virtually all forms of striking use the following basic biomechanical motions to deliver blows:

- Thrusting
- Circular
- Snapping
- Glancing
- Raking
- Slashing

These movements reflect a strike's basic purpose and how force is utilized during the technique. The diagrams shown opposite illustrate these basic biomechanical motions, using arrows to indicate the strike's path.

In *thrusting* strikes, force is focused in a direct line toward the target. Thrusting strikes focus on penetrating or striking through an opponent. A thrusting Side Kick and a Straight Punch are typical examples.

In *circular* strikes, force follows a curved path toward the target. Like thrusting strikes, circular strikes also focus on penetrating or striking through an opponent. A Hook Punch and a Spin Kick are typical examples.

In *snapping* strikes the hand or foot is snapped into the target and quickly retracted upon contact. Depending on technique, snapping strikes may follow either a direct or a circular path to the target. Compared to thrusting strikes, there is less emphasis on hitting through. Snapping hand strikes are usually characterized by an emphasis on lower arm movement (below the elbow). Snapping foot strikes are characterized by an emphasis on lower leg movement (below the knee). A snapping Back Fist Strike and a snapping Side Kick are typical examples.

In *glancing* strikes, the blow glances off the intended target at an angle. Force at impact is directed both forward and sideways. The strike delivery may follow either a direct or a circular path to the target, but always enters and exits at an angle to the surface being struck. Glancing strikes are often used in conjunction with blending movements and can be blocks as well as strikes. A Circular Blade Kick and a Circular Inner-Heel Kick are typical examples.

In *raking* strikes, the blow continues to strike multiple targets in one continuous movement. The hitting motion is similar to a glancing strike, except the attack point continues to strike other targets before deflecting away. The strike may be characterized by either a constant dragging contact, or a series of glancing blows. A Raking Back Fist to the inner arm or a Rising Front Blade Kick to the chest and face are typical examples. Raking strikes may also involve tearing or scratching techniques, such as a Claw Hand to the face.

In *slashing* strikes, a very fast cutting motion parallel to the target is used to cut or abrade the intended target. Slashing strikes are used against the eyes, ears, face, neck, or other soft exposed tissue. The edge of the fingers, fingernails, toes, or shoes are usually used to strike. A Cutting Hand Strike to an opponent's eyes, or a Cutting Crescent Kick to the eyes

or throat, are typical examples. Historically, most slashing strikes evolved by imitating the use of a knife or sword.

Strike Variables
Strikes can be varied or modified in almost limitless ways depending upon variables such as arm/leg position, direction of strike, and amount of force.

Direction of Strike
The direction of a particular strike can be varied in any number of ways, depending upon where the target is located and the intended route for delivering the strike. Within the martial arts world, strike direction is generally characterized using the following terminology. Examples are shown throughout the later chapters outlining strikes.

- Straight
- Outside or Inside
- Outside Circular or Inside Circular
- Rising or Descending
- Angular
- High, Middle, or Low

Straight strikes follow a direct path to the target. Outside strikes follow a horizontal path away from your body. Inside strikes follow a horizontal path toward your body. In circular strikes, the hand or foot follows a circular path (horizontal, vertical, or angular) to the target. Rising and descending strikes follow a vertical motion, while "high, middle, and low" designate a target's height.

Arm/Leg Position and Use
When adopting a fighting stance, strikes may be executed using either the front (leading) or back (guarding) hand, arm, or leg. Generally, lead strikes reach the target faster and are more difficult to block, while rear hand or rear leg strikes take longer to reach the target, but possess greater power due to shoulder and hip rotation assisting the strike. A common tactic in many martial art styles involves use of light, fast lead strikes to set up use of the rear hand or leg. In boxing, this is typified by repeated left jabs used to set up a right cross or uppercut. Lead strikes can also possess great power; however, well timed use of the hips and shoulders is essential.

Strike Mechanics

Thrusting Strike

Circular Strike

Snapping Strike (straight path)

Snapping Strike (circular path)

Glancing Strike

Raking Strike (constant contact)

Raking Strike (series of blows)

Slashing Strike

Methods of Execution

Strikes can be executed singularly, in continuous repetition, in alternating combinations with other strikes or techniques, or in simultaneous combinations with other strikes or techniques.

Single Strikes

Many martial arts are based on the traditional idea that "one punch kills." This theory assumes that one powerful focused strike to a vital target will produce a decisive result (cripple, kill). Subsequent strikes are therefore unnecessary as everything goes into setting up and executing this finishing technique. There is no argument that one punch can be decisive; however, accurately striking a vital target with a single technique when both fighters are moving is easier said than done. There are also many people who can take a great deal of punishment with only marginal effect on their ability to fight, particularly trained fighters or individuals under the influence of drugs. For this reason, many

contemporary martial artists feel it is wiser to practice and apply strikes in fast, continuous combinations, linking strikes to other strikes, blocks, holds, or throws—unless the first blow happens to effectively resolve the situation. Generally, applying strikes in combinations increases the likelihood that one of your blows will connect.

Sequential Strikes

In combination-oriented martial arts, such as Hapkido, strikes are often executed in combinations of two or more strikes delivered in sequence. The first strike is often used to set up the second strike, or subsequent techniques such as holds or throws. Strikes may also be executed in conjunction with, or immediately following, a blocking technique. Basic combination strikes are outlined in a later chapter. Composite techniques linking strikes to blocks, holds, and throws are covered in the author's book, *Hapkido: Traditions, Philosophy, Technique*. A typical sequential combination strike is shown below.

Simultaneous Strikes

It is also possible to execute two or more strikes by using multiple attack points at the same time. Simultaneous strikes can be executed to a range of targets using a variety of techniques, such as punches, elbow strikes, kicks, and butts. These striking techniques are usually referred to as *twin* or *double* strikes. The following simultaneous combinations using two, three, or four body surfaces illustrate the range of possibilities:

- Left Hand, Right Hand
- One Hand, One Leg (opposite sides)
- One Hand, One Leg (same side)
- Both Hands, One Leg
- Both Hands, Both Legs (jumping)
- Left Hand, Right Elbow, Left Leg
- Both Hands, One Leg, Head Butt

Many more combinations are possible depending upon tactics and a given situation. Examples of simultaneous strikes are shown below and on the first page of this chapter.

Single and Combination Strikes

Single Strike (Inside Parry, Ridge Hand Strike)

Sequential Strikes (Grab Parry, Descending Hammer Fist Strike, Inside Crescent Kick)

3 Simultaneous Strikes (twin chop, knee strike)

3 Simultaneous Strikes (Twin Knuckle Hand, Side Kick)

4 Strikes (5-Fingertip Strike, Elbow+Knee Strike, Head Butt)

Feinting

A feint is an intentionally deceptive movement, designed to draw a particular response from your opponent, which you then exploit by executing a predetermined technique. Feinting is used to create an opening for a particular technique which might otherwise be blocked or countered. Feints are also used to draw an opponent's attack (which you know is coming) leaving them vulnerable to your predetermined counterattack. A common feint is to leave a target exposed to draw a specific attack, then countering as your opponent launches their attack. Another common feint involves making a striking motion with the lead hand or leg and attacking with the rear. Feinting can also involve the use of body movements or footwork that cause an opponent to lose their balance, timing, or sense of distance. To be successful, a feint must deceive your opponent causing them to misinterpret the situation. All skilled fighters make use of feints and are adept at recognizing them in their opponents. For this reason, successful feinting has a strong psychological component, in that you are attempting to predict and influence your opponent's responses to perceived attacks or opportunities, without them knowing it. Effective feinting can be compared to skilled acting. If your feint is not convincing, your opponent will recognize it for *what it is,* instead of *what it is not.*

Traditional vs Modern Execution

Historically, the strikes of many martial arts were characterized by certain ideals regarding use of the body to support the strike. When observing traditional striking forms in many martial arts, one would often notice: pronounced hip and shoulder rotation for power and reach; strike extension past the target surface for penetrating power (rather than snapping back); and use of circular strikes with long deliveries designed to increase power by increasing hand or foot velocity. During the last three decades of the twentieth century, many arts began to evolve at a very rapid rate, with deliveries becoming much shorter and more biomechanically efficient. Consequently, in modern fighting and self-defense, long traditional deliveries are only practical when executing finishing blows to stunned opponents, or when the target is well set up and chances of a counterstrike is unlikely. Otherwise, long deliveries are easily avoided and can leave one vulnerable to counters. Nonetheless, traditional movements are still used during training in many schools, to develop speed, timing, coordination, and power. When applied to practical self-defense, long, full motions become abbreviated as required. Remember, it is easy to shorten your technique, but unless you understand and practice the principles of a fully developed strike, your shortened movements will fail to articulate the supporting body movements essential for speed and power. Short deliveries use the same principles as long deliveries, only are more economical in motion. Comparisons are shown below and on the next page.

Traditional vs Modern Execution

Traditional Striking Form (long delivery, pronounced body movement, deep stance, extended follow-through)

Modern Striking Form (short delivery, economized body movement, narrow stance, quick return to guard)

Strike Selection

Many of the strikes outlined in this section are an important part of Hapkido, as well as of many other martial arts. Other strikes are rarely used, except in very specific situations. Strike usage is clarified in the detailed descriptions found in subsequent chapters.

Strikes should be selected based upon: who you are, what you do well, what you are likely to use, and how much damage you are psychologically comfortable inflicting on another individual. The needs of a 95 pound woman defending herself against overpowering opponents are very different than the needs of a 275 pound policeman who needs to restrain individuals without unduly injuring them. Further contrast this with the needs of a professional soldier who wishes to immobilize or kill the opposition in the simplest, most expedient manner. Evaluate your needs, select the appropriate range of strikes, and emphasize training as required.

It is quite rare for an individual to master use of all the strike techniques outlined in this book. Decades of training are required and success is never assured. Certain physical limitations or body characteristics may also make this impractical. As your training progresses, you will develop a preference for certain strike techniques over others. This is common and desirable. The development of favorite techniques and procedures is part of the evolution of any martial artist.

Less is More

Today, many schools do not even teach the vast majority of strikes historically associated with their style. Instead they focus on fewer well-proven techniques, which are easier to learn and more likely to be executed properly in high-stress situations such as self-defense or combat. It is worth noting that many great fighters and martial artists use relatively few techniques, but become highly accomplished in those that they use.

More is More

An alternate point of view: The more you learn, the greater the reservoir of knowledge and technique you have to draw from. This is particularly important in improvisation. In the flow of a fight, the opportunity to use techniques you never thought of using may seem to appear out of nowhere—only because you have practiced and programmed your body through constant repetition. In certain circumstances, a rarely used strike may constitute the only practical response. Remember, you never know how a situation will develop or what particular opportunities or limitations will emerge.

For example, what happens if your hand becomes damaged and you can no longer clench your fist? Are you fluent in those "rarely used" open-hand strikes which might be substituted for the same purpose? You'd better hope so. In the beginning, practice everything. At a later date, who knows what you may wish or need to use? You never know and you can never guess, so be prepared.

Strikes to Pressure Points

In many martial arts, strikes are directed to highly sensitive nerves or pressure points located throughout the body. This is thought to be a more efficient manner of striking, since less force is needed to affect an opponent. This is also very useful when smaller persons are confronting overpowering opponents.

When striking pressure points, the Fore Fist or other attack points with larger contact areas are less frequently used, since the broader surface area is felt to diminish a strike's effectiveness by spreading force out over a larger area. When striking pressure points, this often results in damaging the surrounding tissue without actually affecting the pressure point itself. Power is far more concentrated or focused by employing attack points using very small surfaces, such as the finger knuckles or the tips of fingers and toes. This relation of "force to attack point size" is better understood by comparing the strike of a broad hammer with the blow from a nail.

Traditional vs Modern Execution

Traditional Roundhouse Kick (long delivery commencing from side, pronounced hip rotation, simultaneous blocks)

Modern Roundhouse Kick (short delivery, chamber with knee pointing forward)

Strikes to pressure points can involve a single strike to a single point, a single strike to a group of points, or a series of strikes to related points. Effects include localized pain, numbness, partial paralysis, weakness, loss of breathing, or loss of consciousness. The effect obtained depends upon the particular point or series of points struck, the degree of force, angle of attack, and individual sensitivity. Sensitivity is related to musculature, fat content, and cyclical timing (see *Essential Anatomy for Healing and Martial Arts* by the same author). Targeting pressure points requires *extreme* accuracy, as the actual target is usually the size of a dime or less. The angle of attack is also very important, since many points can only be effectively hit from a single direction. Light to medium force strikes are usually powerful enough to be effective. However, if you miss the point and the surrounding area is anatomically strong, your blow is essentially useless.

Today, many martial artists suggest striking *forcefully* (not lightly) to pressure points in anatomically weak or highly vulnerable areas that do not require pinpoint accuracy (e.g., elbow, knees, jaw, temple). For example, if you strike to the Triple Warmer-17 point at the back of the jaw, using a light blow at the correct angle (back to front), you may cause a loss of consciousness for reasons that are as yet unclear. If you are striking with light force and you miss the point, your blow is likely useless. If you strike with greater force, missing the target really doesn't matter, since you will either dislocate or fracture the jaw, induce whiplash, traumatize local nerves, or at the very least cause considerable pain.

Training and Conditioning

It is important to strike targets, punching mitts, and bags that closely approximate the density, texture, and weight of the human targets you are likely to strike. Only by rigorous training and conditioning of striking surfaces and body parts will you obtain the skill and confidence to execute strikes without damage to your own bones and joints. Thousands of repetitions are recommended. An improperly executed punch can easily break your wrist, knuckles, or fingers. Safe, powerful, controlled strikes rely on strengthened striking surfaces, as well as well-trained wrists and ankles.

Common Injuries

Most injuries to attack points occur as a result of improper striking technique, striking too forcefully, or use of the strike point in an inappropriate manner. Careful preparation and training mixed with common sense can prevent most injuries. The importance of developing an awareness of your own limitations cannot be overemphasized. For further information concerning probable causes, prevention, and rehabilitation for common martial arts injuries, refer to one of the many comprehensive texts available on sports medicine and training.

Skin Callus

Some skin callus is desirable to protect the tissue on attacking surfaces such as the fist and foot. This callus is usually formed during the normal course of training. Shaving the callus periodically will keep its size under control. To prevent drying and cracking, keep callused skin moist with heavy moisturizing emollients or petroleum jelly.

Bone Callus

The ability to hit hard without breaking bone depends on numerous factors, including bone mass and elasticity. Specific conditioning to strengthen bone was common practice for centuries, but is less prevalent today due to adverse effects associated with the training. Historically, bone conditioning was very important for a warrior. To be an effective weapon, a punch needed to pierce wooden armor. Unconditioned bone was considered a liability. Today, the major reason for bone conditioning is to demonstrate breaking skills.

Although bone can be marginally strengthened through nutrition, only the building of bone callus can significantly alter bone mass. Traditionally, bone callus is built up by repeated light striking to a very hard surface (such as wood or iron). The bone is repeatedly bruised, and the body repairs the bruised bone by forming additional bone in the damaged area. The process is constantly repeated as new layers of bone build upon existing bone, gradually increasing bone mass and thickness at the strike point.

Bone conditioning should only be done under expert supervision, gradually, over a period of years. Anyone involved in bone conditioning should also expect significant long-term negative health effects to the surrounding joints. Arthritis is common, and incidents of bone cancer have been reported.

Responsible Use of Force

Martial techniques should only be used for self-defense, the protection of others, physical exercise, or in organized sport competition between consenting individuals. The use of force to resolve a situation carries with it a social and moral responsibility to apply force in an appropriate and sensible manner.

The purpose of a strike is to deter, damage, cripple, or kill your opponent. The amount of force and the target selected greatly influence the degree of destruction. Be aware of the difference between a *nuisance* and a *life threatening* situation. Use only the force required to safely resolve a situation without endangering yourself. Not all confrontations require the use of strikes. Often a simple restraining technique or hold will suffice.

When you resolve to strike, do so with purpose and decisiveness. A few quick strikes which demonstrate your abilities can often convince an opponent to abandon an attack, resulting in less damage to you, less damage to your opponent, and less likelihood of a lawsuit. Remember, it's easy to seriously injure or kill someone, with a minimum of skills. It may not be as easy to live with what you have done. Your skill and maturity are shown by how little force you require, not how hard you can hit. For the skilled martial artist, the *excessive use of force* is an inexcusable and morally reprehensible act, deserving condemnation.

Comparing Martial Arts

The photos on the following four pages show examples of similar strikes from different martial arts, as they are applied by notable masters. In some cases, the differences are obvious; others require a more educated eye or prior experience with specific styles to be able to perceive the subtle distinctions that distinguish one art from another.

The purpose of these photos is not to make any particular point, but to invite the reader to look outside of their own art. Understanding how other martial arts interpret similar techniques can lead one to a deeper understanding of their own art, and its place in the larger culture of martial arts. Please recognize that these photos have been selected for their similarities. Each of these martial arts also possess numerous qualities and techniques that are relatively unique unto themselves. Please do not assume that by looking at these photos you understand these arts. To make in-depth comparisons and draw intelligent conclusions would require the examination of hundreds of techniques, decades of training, and a great deal of familiarity with specific martial arts.

Hapkido: *Inside Parry / Middle-Finger-Fist Punch / Inside Elbow Strike with arm lock and trap, as demonstrated by the author in his book* Hapkido: Traditions, Philosophy, Technique

Taekwondo: *Inside Block / Reverse Straight Punch, as demonstrated by Sihak Henry Cho in his book* Taekwondo: Secrets of Korean Karate, *1968*

Karate: *Rising Block / Reverse Punch, as demonstrated in the book* Karate-Do Kyohan: The Master Text *by Gichin Funakoshi, 1973 (first published in 1936)*

Aikido: *A portion of Ikkyo with Atemi (The First Movement with Strike to Pressure Point) as demonstrated by Mitsugi Saotome in his book* The Principles of Aikido, *1989*

Wing Chun Kung Fu: *Grabbing Hand Block / Punch / Slap Block / Punch, as demonstrated by William Cheung in his book* Advanced Wing Chun, *1988*

Kuk Sool Won: *Rising Block / Knife Hand Parry / Straight Punch, as demonstrated by He-Young Kimm in his book* Kuk Sool: Korean Martial Arts, *1985*

Jeet Kune Do: *Lead Feint / Rear Straight Punch, as demonstrated by Bruce Lee in his book* Bruce Lee's Fighting Method: Advanced Techniques (coauthor M. Uyehara), *1966*

Hapkido: *Turning Back Side Kick / Grab Parry / Inside Crescent Kick, as demonstrated by the author in his book* Hapkido: Traditions, Philosophy, Technique

Taekwondo: *Side Thrust Kick / Front Snap Kick, as demonstrated by Hee Il Cho in his book* The Complete Martial Artist: Volume 2, *1981*

Karate: *Hooking Block / Side Thrust Kick, as demonstrated by Masatoshi Nakayama in his book* Dynamic Karate, *1966*

Muay Thai Kick-Boxing: *Leg Block / Roundhouse Kick, as demonstrated by Walter Michalowski in CFW's* Combat Fitness *magazine, 2001*

Wing Chun Kung Fu: *Thrusting Hand Block / Side Kick with Heel, as demonstrated by William Cheung in his book* Advanced Wing Chun, *1988*

Hwa Rang Do: *Inside Full-Moon Kick / Side Kick, as demonstrated by Hwa Rang Do founder Lee-Joo Bang in his book* The Ancient Martial Art of Hwa Rang Do: Vol. 1, *1978*

Kuk Sool Won: *X Block / Wrist Grab / Side Kick, as demonstrated by He-Young Kimm in his book* Kuk Sool: Korean Martial Arts, *1985*

Jeet Kune Do: *Lead Feint / Lead Side Kick, as demonstrated by Bruce Lee in his book* Bruce Lee's Fighting Method: Advanced Techniques (coauthor M. Uyehara), *1966*

When building a house, one begins with the foundation. If the foundation is strong, the building's structure will be able to withstand the trials of nature and time. If the foundation is weak, the entire structure will be undermined, and its life span more limited. Before learning and practicing specific martial strikes, it is important to first understand the basic principles that govern the execution of virtually all striking techniques. A proper grasp of fundamentals and basic skills will allow practitioners to learn more quickly, refine their

FUNDAMENTALS

skills to a higher degree, enjoy their training, and avoid the unnecessary injuries commonly resulting from improperly executed strikes. The process of learning to strike, and to block and avoid, should not be painful or injurious, but rather a physically robust, confidence-building experience that leaves one exhilarated and looking forward to more training. This chapter will outline basic principles and techniques, all of which must be learned from a qualified instructor to ensure that your martial arts training is safe and rewarding.

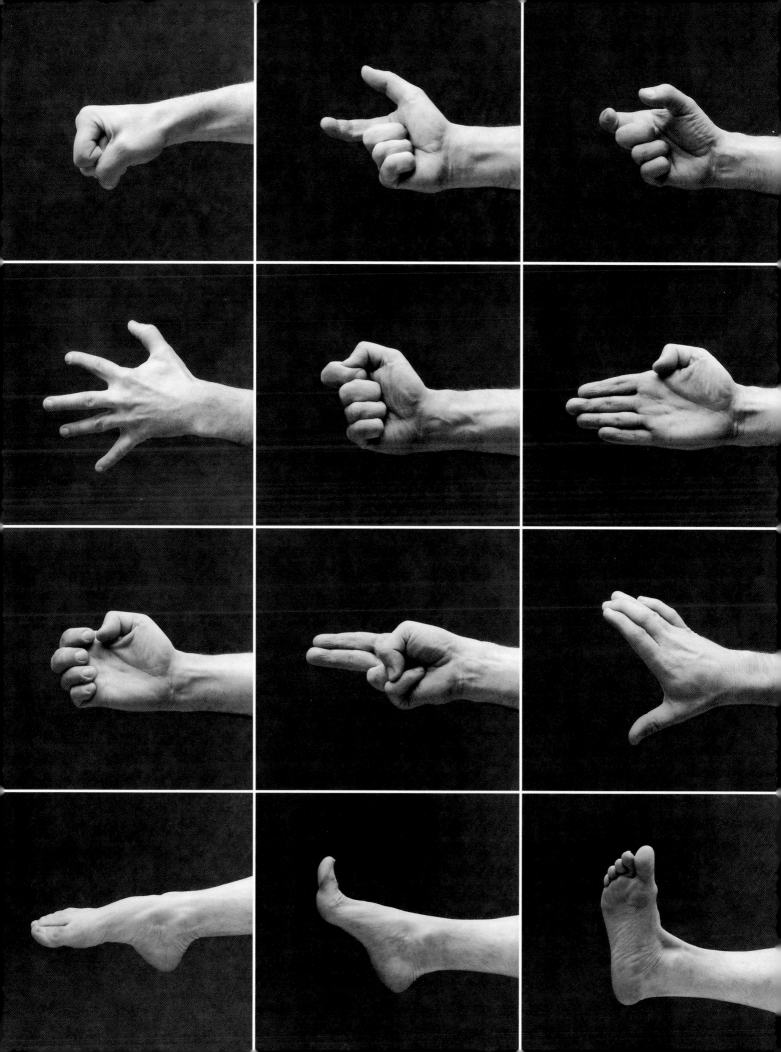

Ki

The word *Ki* (also written as *Qi, Chi, or Gi*) is essentially untranslatable, although it is often described as the "vital energy" or "life force" that permeates the universe, flowing through and animating all things. It has been the basis of Oriental medicine for thousands of years.

In martial arts, the combative use of Ki usually involves blending and harmonizing your own Ki (internal energy) with that of your opponent and the greater universe. This is done to assist the application of a technique, such as a strike, hold, throw, or escape. Although skillful technique does not require Ki manipulation to be highly effective, focusing Ki will increase a technique's efficiency. When fighting a highly skilled or overpowering opponent, harmonized Ki may be the difference between a technique that works and one that fails. In energy-oriented martial arts, such as Hapkido, Aikido, and Tai Chi Chuan, one's ability to strengthen and control Ki is developed through exercises and meditation. For serious practitioners trying to develop their Ki, a variety of factors must be in balance—diet, air quality, emotional state, sleep, sexual activity, and the level of stress in your life all affect the levels of Ki in your body.

Live-Hand

The term *Live-Hand* refers to specific hand formations which are used in the martial art Hapkido to increase the flow of Ki into the hands and arms. This increases arm strength and power when most needed, such as during a wrist escape or the execution of a strike.

Live-Hand techniques involve visualization, breath control, and tensing of the fingers, hands, and arms. Concentration and focus are very important, as is practice. The use of a Live-Hand is typically characterized by extending one or more fingers and breathing out as a specific technique is applied.

As previously stated, the techniques in this book come from Hapkido; thus, one will notice the use of Live-Hands in many techniques. If you practice a martial art that does not use Live-Hands, merely ignore that portion of the technique. Live-Hands are not a crucial component of the strikes and blocks shown, but rather one of the useful additions that can create greater efficiency.

In recent years, the use of extended fingers in combat has fallen into disfavor among some practitioners due to their increased vulnerability to attack or damage. Today many stylists restrict Live-Hand use in fighting to wrist escapes, well-controlled breaking blocks, or holds in which the extra power is often needed and the fingers are well-protected from being grabbed or broken.

Typical Live-Hand Formations

The photographs shown below illustrate two typical Live-Hand formations. In the lower-left photographs, a basic Live-Hand is formed by spreading all five fingers very wide, with the thumb slightly bent. This hand formation expands and hardens the wrist and forearm, concentrating Ki in the hand and fingertips.

It is often used to apply wrist escapes, blocks, and arm strikes. In the lower-right photos, a Live-Hand is formed by closing the hand, with only the forefinger extended (in some techniques, the thumb is also extended). This formation is often used when gripping limbs or executing a Hammer Fist strike.

Breath Control

Proper breathing when executing techniques is essential. Do not hold your breath. During training or combat, try to breathe deeply and rhythmically. This calms the mind, oxygenates the blood, and maximizes the flow of Ki throughout the body, encouraging peak performance. In most martial arts, you will exhale as a technique is applied or a strike is executed. This helps coordinate physical actions, increases physical strength, and channels Ki to the extremities; it is is often referred to as *breath power* or *extending one's Ki*. Conceptually, three actions (breathing, physical action, and the flow of Ki from one's center to the limbs) become one coordinated, powerful response. When these actions are intimately linked to an opponent's energies and actions, technique becomes effortless.

The Energy-Shout

The distinct shout many martial artists emit when executing techniques is essentially breathing meditation converted to dynamic action. In Korean, this energy harmonizing shout is referred to as a *Kihap*. In the Japanese language it is called a *Kiai*. Most Chinese arts do not use an audible shout.

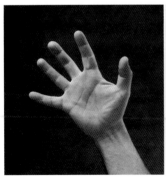

Live-Hand with five fingers spread (executing a Rising Elbow Strike)

Live-Hand with forefinger extended (executing a Hammer Fist strike to pressure points)

The word *Ki* is defined as the universal energy or dynamic force that animates all things. *Hap* or *Ai* is the root form for words which connote harmonizing, coming together, or coordinating. Thus the concept of *Kihap* or *Kiai* literally means to harmonize with the dynamic universal life force. The "energy-harmonizing shout" is a means, then, of coordinating our actions with the flow of energies and events of which we are part. All individual actions and events merge into a single flow. This is what is meant by "being at one with the universe."

The Dynamic Release of Energy
When you execute a punch, kick, hold, or throw, or block a strike, energy is released—typically as a rush of air from the lungs. This exhalation of air, coordinated with muscular tension in the body and throat, creates the deep, roaring growl of the true energy-shout. When you are first learning martial arts, the energy-shout will mostly be an artificial adornment, merely accompanying physical actions. However, if you train in an uninhibited way, focusing on the purpose of the shout, you will eventually develop a shout that is natural, spontaneous, and uninhibited. It will become a reflection of your dynamic emotional state, and an expression of the harmonized, total commitment of your body, mind, and spirit to the techniques you are executing. The true energy-shout is often characterized as a low, deep, harsh roar that emerges from the diaphragm, rather than the throat. It should be an expression of indomitable spirit, not fright.

The Silent Shout
The silent shout is not an audible shout, but rather a total commitment of body, mind, emotions, and spirit into the events of the moment. There is no thought of the outcome, only the now. You are completely in tune with your opponent's actions. The silent shout is considered to be the highest level of energy-harmonizing. If there is any sound at all, it might be characterized as a low humming "ohmm" sound, which is a reflection of your own breathing in unison with the events transpiring before you. Remember, the ultimate objective is not to make noise, but to develop a natural and effortless unification of body, mind, and spirit.

Leading and Blending
Leading refers to the act of directing your opponent into a strike, hold, or throw by using their own energy against them. This may involve redirecting a strike or charge, or creating an initially deceptive movement that causes your opponent to react by moving in a direction that assists the execution of your technique. Leading movements can be short or long depending on circumstances, and are often executed in the opposite direction in which you intend your opponent to move. For example, if you pull an opponent's arm toward your right, they will usually react by pulling to your left. This sets up specific techniques.

Blending refers to the act of uniting with your opponent's force. This reduces your chances of injury and increases the efficiency of your

techniques, by avoiding a direct confrontation with your opponent's forces. Blending can be thought of metaphorically, as occupying the calm space within a tornado, or joining with the force of the tornado by matching its speed and motion. This is accomplished by knowing when to give way and when to attack. Blending is particularly important when countering with holds or throws, or facing an overpowering opponent. In practical terms, leading and blending require good footwork, timing, speed, power, and versatility, as demonstrated in the photo sequence below.

Pressure Point Attacks
Some martial arts, such as Hapkido, make extensive use of pressure points (also called *acupoints*) to assist the application of techniques, including strikes. These are the same points commonly used in Eastern medicine to heal the human body. Manipulating pressure points alters the body's energetic state by affecting Ki-flow and neurological functions. In martial arts, specific pressure points may be struck or pressed to cause pain; reduce physical strength; cause involuntary muscle responses; limit motor functions; cause loss of consciousness; or damage neurological, respiratory, or circulatory functions. In striking techniques, pressure point attacks are mostly used to increase the efficiency of a strike, decrease power requirements, and reduce the likelihood of injuries. In this book, pressure points are cited using their standard alpha-numeric name (e.g., TW-11). Common points are shown at the end of this chapter.

Leading, blending, breath control, and complete harmony with an attacker's energy are demonstrated in an avoiding and counterstriking technique.

Overview

Attack points are the specific parts of your body (hands, feet, elbows, knees, head, etc.) which are used to attack specific targets and execute specific techniques. The method of attack is usually a strike; however, these same body surfaces are often used when applying joint locks, chokes, throws, and pins. The use of a particular attack point usually involves specific formations of the hand, foot, or other parts of the body.

Sixty attack points commonly used in Hapkido and other martial arts are described on the following pages. The use of these formations in specific striking and kicking techniques is outlined in the appropriate chapters covering these techniques. There are also a number of other attack points and body surfaces that are used in specialized applications, or are found in specific martial arts styles. It should be remembered that almost any part of the body can be an effective weapon with proper training and an appropriate situation.

Effects of Clothing

Most martial arts are practiced with bare hands and feet in a martial arts uniform. The nature and effectiveness of a particular attack point often changes when it is covered with normal clothing, or padded for competition. For example, elbow strikes beneath heavy jackets quickly lose their effectiveness based on the amount of padding. Shoes or boots can provide considerable benefit to certain kicking techniques, while diminishing the power of others. Wearing bulky winter gloves will make hand attacks to highly sensitive nerve points a virtual impossibility.

There is no question that wearing normal clothing places specific limitations on technique. Therefore, it is extremely important to train for a variety of situations so that confidence and a real understanding of technique limits is clearly grasped by the practitioner. A well-rounded approach to attack point use will provide valuable options for real-life situations.

Safe Use of Force

Generally, the more muscle tissue there is surrounding the bone, the harder you can strike or press without injury to yourself. The amount of force which can be safely generated behind a particular strike varies individually, and is usually based on the following factors:

- Size of bone
- Strength of bone
- Amount of muscle surrounding bone
- Strength of supporting musculature
- Nerve sensitivity
- Hardness of target
- Movement of target after impact

Power Attacks

The most powerful attack points (based on ability to sustain impact without damage) in descending order are:

- Bottom Heel
- Lower Elbow
- Forearm
- Hammer Fist
- Upper Elbow
- Palm Heel
- Bent Wrist

Soft Tissue Attacks

The following attack points are generally used to attack soft tissue, tendons, muscles, or nerves. Their vulnerability to damage makes them inappropriate for use in hard strikes unless special conditioning is undertaken.

- Index Finger Fist
- Middle Finger Fist
- Knuckle Fist
- Knuckle Hand
- Chicken Hand
- Spear Hand
- Five Fingertip Hand
- Tiger Mouth Hand
- Thumb Hand
- Pincer Hand
- Head
- Chin

Attack Point Selection

Many strikes, holds, or pressing attacks can be executed using a variety of different attack points for the same technique. Try to use the attack point which most efficiently corresponds to the target size, shape, and degree to which the target is exposed or protected. In many situations, this takes little more than simple observation and a basic knowledge of anatomy.

For example, a Side Kick directed to the solar plexus should use the Bottom Heel, since the shape of this attack point corresponds with the opening at the base of sternum. A Side Kick to the throat is more effective when using a Knife Foot attack point, since the long thin hitting surface provides greater penetration, slips under the chin should an opponent drop the head, and reduces the negative effects of an inaccurate strike.

When targeting nerves, pressure points, eyes, or other very small targets, a small penetrating attack point such as the Middle Finger Fist or Spear Hand is most practical. Striking well-protected nerves with a Fore Fist or Back Hand would likely damage the surrounding area while leaving the nerve itself untouched.

Forming Attack Points

The use of a particular attack point involves specific formations of the hand, foot, arm, leg, or other body parts. This is shown and described on the following pages. However, a qualified teacher is essential to assure proper formation and use. Otherwise injury may result from surfaces which are poorly formed, or used for inappropriate purposes.

For example, when executing many hand strikes, the precise placement of the fingers, muscle tensioning, hand-to-wrist alignment, hand-to-target orientation, degree of force, and use of the hips and shoulders are all extremely important in assuring maximum efficiency and protecting your hitting surfaces from damage. Poorly formed attack points may end up causing more damage to yourself than to the opponent you strike.

Forming a Fist

A clenched fist is one of the most common hand formations used in striking. There are two basic methods of forming a fist. The first method is currently used throughout the martial arts world. The second method was in common use until the mid-twentieth century, but is rarely seen today. It use declined because it was more difficult to form and the little finger is comparatively looser. However, it focuses greater tension in the upper fingers and retracts the second index knuckle further inward, which is a more protected position. This is useful for individuals with anatomically longer index fingers, who may have trouble folding the index finger in tightly. Both methods provide excellent results if one is well-practiced and accustomed to using the technique. In both versions the fingers are tightly wrapped into a ball for maximum protection during strikes.

These two methods of forming fists are shown at right. Once this is grasped, forming other closed hand formations (outlined on the following pages) will be much easier.

Forming a Knife Foot

The Knife Foot may be formed in one of three ways, which are shown below. In all three versions the hitting surface is the same; only the arrangement of the foot varies. The first option, "curling the toes downward," is the oldest method and makes it easier to tighten the foot. The second option, "curling the toes upward," is more modern and permits greater flexibility in the ankle. Today, this version is commonly seen in many martial arts styles. The third option, "small toes downward with big toe up," probably evolved in an attempt to combine the virtues of the other two formations. Be aware that some individuals may be unable to form the toes in this manner due to anatomical irregularities or previous injuries.

All three methods work equally well, although the third version is preferred by many martial artists for stylistic reasons. Experiment to determine what works best for you.

Attack Point Selection

Left: Attack points with larger surfaces are used to distribute force over a broad area. A Back Hand Strike is shown.

Right: Attack points with small surfaces are used to concentrate force at a specific point. A Spear Hand Strike to both eyes is shown.

Forming a Fist

*Method 1:
Place fingertips at base of fingers, close and press fingers tightly against palm. Wrap thumb over index and middle fingers and press. Make sure little finger is not relaxed.*

*Method 2:
Wrap 3 fingers tightly against palm. Wrap index over middle finger. Wrap thumb over index finger and press downward. Make sure little finger is not relaxed or loose.*

Forming a Knife Foot

*Method 1:
Toes curled downward.*

*Method 2:
Toes curled upward.*

*Method 3:
Toes curled down, big toe up.*

Fore Fist

Purpose: Strike, press.

Typical use: Punch, choke.

Formed by tightly closing and clenching four fingers with thumb pressing down against index and middle finger. Contact area is front of first two knuckles when striking, or all 4 knuckles when pressing.

Back Fist

Purpose: Strike, press.

Typical use: Punch to temple or ribs. Formed same as a Fore Fist. Contact area is back of the hand and tops of first two knuckles. The two smaller knuckles can also be used for hitting, usually for lightly striking acupoints in awkward locations.

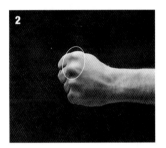

Hammer Fist

Purpose: Strike.

Typical use: Punch to head, ribs. Formed same as Fore Fist. Contact area is bottom fleshy part of fist. The knuckles of little finger can also be used for hitting (if fist is angled), usually for striking acupoints. Also called *Bottom Fist* or *Iron Hammer.*

Loose Hammer Fist

Purpose: Strike.

Typical use: Punch to head, ribs. Same as Hammer Fist only leave index finger and thumb relaxed and partially open. Used to increase Ki-flow and keep arm more relaxed for greater speed. Contact area same as Hammer Fist. Also called *Edge Fist.*

Ki Hammer Fist

Purpose: Strike.

Typical use: Punch to head, ribs. Formed same as Loose Hammer Fist only extend partially bent index finger and thumb to increase Ki-flow and keep arm more relaxed for greater speed. Contact area is the same as Hammer Fist.

Thumb Fist

Purpose: Strike, press, choke.

Typical use: Punch to temple, ribs. Formed same as Fore Fist only with protruding thumb pressing down against side of index finger for support. Contact area is point of, or area between, thumb knuckles. Also used in place of Fore Fist.

Middle Finger Fist

Purpose: Strike, press.

Typical use: Punch, release hold. Fist with second knuckle of middle finger extended. Tightly wrap thumb over index and middle finger, use adjacent fingers for support. For pin-point attacks to nerves or protected areas. Contact is at point of knuckle.

Index Finger Fist

Purpose: Strike, press, choke.

Typical use: Punch, release hold. Formed same as Fore Fist only extend second knuckle of index finger and brace on side with thumb. Same purpose as Middle Finger Fist. Often used in place of Middle Finger Fist if fist cannot be tightly clenched.

Knuckle Fist

Purpose: Strike, press.

Typical use: Uppercut Punch, choke. Formed same as Thumb Fist. Used for strikes to soft areas, or pressing nerve attacks. Cannot withstand same impact as Fore Fist without hand damage. Contact area is points of second set of four knuckles.

Knuckle Hand

Purpose: Strike, press.

Typical use: Strike to throat or ribs. Formed by bending and pressing fingertips inward against palm, with hand slightly bent. Bend and press thumb against index finger, or fold back into palm (more protected). Contact area is same as Knuckle Fist.

Knife Hand
Purpose: Strike, block, press.
Typical use: Strike to throat.
Formed by extending fingers with slight bend at second knuckles. Press fingers tightly together, press bent thumb against palm, tense hand and wrist. Contact area is fleshy edge of tensed hand.

Cutting Hand
Purpose: Slashing or cutting strike.
Typical use: Slash to eyes or throat.
Formed same as Knife Hand. Used to cut or scratch sensitive targets such as eyes, ears, nose, lips and neck. Effective as a distraction, or to set up another technique. Contact area is tips and nails of fingers.

Relaxed Back Hand
Purpose: Strike, block.
Typical use: Thrusting strike to face.
Fingers and wrist remain loose and relaxed to encourage speed and fluidity. Used primarily in fast strike combinations to sensitive targets such as the face, temple, and ribs. Contact area is back of hand.

Tense Back Hand
Purpose: Strike, block.
Typical use: Circular strike, parry.
Formed same as Knife Hand. Hand and wrist are rigidly tensed and aligned. Used primarily in soft blocks and parries. Also used to strike soft or sensitive targets. Contact area is back of the hand.

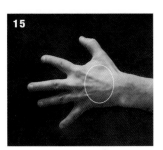

Ki Back Hand
Purpose: Strike, block.
Typical use: Circular strike to ribs.
Similar to a Tense Back Hand, except fingers are spread with thumb slightly bent, in a Live-Hand formation. Used to increase Ki-flow into hand, when striking or blocking. Contact area is back of the hand.

Spear Hand
Purpose: Strike, press, choke.
Typical use: Strike to throat, groin.
Formed like a Knife Hand with middle finger more bent, so three fingertips form an even edge. Used to attack solar plexus, throat, armpit, or other soft vulnerable targets. Contact area is the tips of the first three fingers.

Spear Hand – 2 Fingers
Purpose: Strike, press, choke.
Typical use: Strike to base of throat.
Formed by rigidly extending fore and middle fingers. For hard strikes, flex fingers slightly. Used for pinpoint attacks to nerves or soft protected areas such as eyes or throat. Contact area is the first two fingertips.

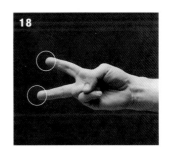

Spear Hand – 2 Fingers Spread
Purpose: Strike, press.
Typical use: Strike to both eyes.
Formed by rigidly extending and spreading index and middle fingers. Used for pinpoint attacks to two nerves or soft protected areas such as both eyes. Contact area is the first two fingertips.

Spear Hand – 1 Finger
Purpose: Strike, press.
Typical use: Strike to eye, throat.
Formed by rigidly extending forefinger, clenching other fingers like a Fore Fist. Used for pinpoint attacks to nerves or soft protected areas such as eyes or throat. Contact area is the first two fingertips.

Ridge Hand
Purpose: Strike, block, press.
Typical use: Strike to throat, neck.
Formed same as Knife Hand, tuck thumb further in against palm, inner edge of hand is tensed. Contact area extends from slightly below base of index finger to first thumb joint. Also called *Inner Edge Hand.*

ATTACK POINTS

Ox Jaw Hand
Purpose: Strike, block, press.
Typical use: Block punch at biceps.
Formed same as Knife Hand with hand bent sideways at wrist. Outside edge of hand and wrist form a curve. Used to strike collarbone or face, block a strike, or apply pressure. Contact area is same as Knife Hand.

Bear Hand
Purpose: Strike.
Typical use: Strike to side of head. Formed by bending and pressing fingertips inward against palm, stretching palm to tighten striking surface. Used for striking a broad area. Contact area is entire palm and fingertips. Also called *Bear Paw*.

Chicken Hand
Purpose: Strike, block, press.
Typical use: Strike to armpit, neck. Formed same as Knife Hand with fingers and thumb flexed slightly inward. Wrist bent opposite of Ox Jaw Hand. Wrist is bent or snapped during strike or block. Contact area is base and first joint of thumb.

Claw Hand
Purpose: Rake, tear, grab.
Typical use: Clawing eyes or ears. Formed by bending 5 fingertips partially inward imitating a claw. Used for scratching and tearing soft or protruding tissue and clothing. Contact area is tips and nails of all five fingers. Also called *Tiger Claw*.

Tiger Mouth Hand
Purpose: Strike, press, hold.
Typical use: Strike or clamping hold to throat. Form Knife Hand with thumb widely separated. Also used to apply pressure in wrist locks. Contact area is between tip of thumb and first knuckle of index finger. Also called *Circle Hand* or *Circle Ridge*.

Five Fingertip Hand
Purpose: Thrusting strike.
Typical use: Strike to face, groin. Formed by partially bending all five fingertips inward. Similar to Claw Hand with fingers more extended. Used for strikes to nerve clusters or multiple targets over a broad area. Contact area is all five fingertips.

Palm Heel Hand
Purpose: Strike, block, press.
Typical use: Strike to chin. Formed same as Knife Hand with hand bent back at wrist. Wrist is snapped during strikes to chest, ribs, head, temple, jaw, and nose. Also used to apply holds or for blocking. Contact area is at base of palm.

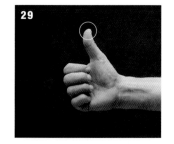

Thumb Hand
Purpose: Strike, gouge, press.
Typical use: Gouge eyes, choke. Form a loosely clenched fist with thumb extended (locked or bent). Used to strike or press exposed nerves, release a hold, or gouge while gripping (e.g., Thumb Hand Choke). Contact area is tip of thumb.

Open Hand
Purpose: Strike, block, press.
Typical use: Puncture eardrums. Formed like Knife Hand with hand sometimes cupped. Hand may be relaxed or tense, with wrist straight or bent, depending upon technique. Used to strike, slap, push, block, or hold. Contact area is entire palm.

Pincer Hand
Purpose: Strike, press, hold, choke.
Typical use: Strike to Adam's apple. Form by bending thumb and forefinger while clenching other three fingers. For clamping strikes, chokes, and holds to two nerves. Contact area is tip of forefinger and thumb, and sometimes three knuckles.

Eagle Hand

Purpose: Strike.

Typical use: Strike to ribs, temple. Formed by tightly compressing five fingertips together. Snap hand forward at wrist during strike (like a bird using its beak). Contact area is tips of all five fingers. Also called *Peacock Hand* or *Eagle's Beak.*

Bent Wrist

Purpose: Strike, block.

Typical use: Strike to groin. Formed like an Eagle Hand, except fingers and hand are relaxed. Snap wrist forward during strike. Often used as a disguised strike or block during a walking movement. Contact area is top of bent wrist.

Inner Wrist

Purpose: Strike, press, hold, choke.

Typical use: Naked Choke. Formed by bending wrist and protruding inner wrist bone. Often used to strike neck, press nerves during holds, or apply chokes to carotid artery or windpipe. Contact area is head of radius bone.

Outer Wrist

Purpose: Strike, press, hold.

Typical use: Lapel Choke, arm bar. Formed by bending wrist and protruding outer wrist bone. Often used to strike neck, press nerves during holds, or apply chokes to carotid artery or windpipe. Contact area is head of ulna bone.

Inner Forearm

Purpose: Strike, block, press.

Typical use: Outside Block, choke. Forearm should be tensed by using open or closed hand formations. Used for strikes, hard blocks, holds, and chokes. Contact area is along radius bone (thumb side) between inner wrist and inner elbow.

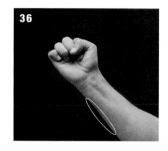

Outer Forearm

Purpose: Strike, block, press.

Typical use: Strike to throat, arm bar. Forearm should be tensed by using open or closed hand formations (stepped hand shown). Used for strikes, blocks, and holds. Contact area is along ulna bone (pinky side) between wrist and elbow.

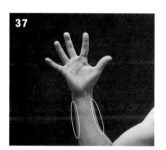

Live-Hand Forearm

Purpose: Strike, block, escape holds.

Typical use: Forearm Arm Bar. A Live-Hand is used to expand wrist, tense forearm and increase Ki-flow. Used for forearm strikes, blocks, holds, or to escape a wrist hold. Contact area is along radius or ulna bone between wrist and elbow.

Upper Elbow

Purpose: Strike, press.

Typical use: Back strike to ribs. Tense muscles near elbow point by using open or closed hand formations. Used for power strikes to any target on the body. Contact area is bone and muscle near point of elbow.

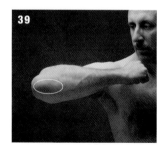

Lower Elbow

Purpose: Strike, press.

Typical use: Rising strike to chin. Tense muscles near elbow point by using open or closed hand formations. Used for power strikes to any target on the body. Contact is at bone and muscle near point of elbow (stronger than Upper Elbow).

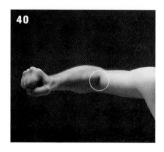

Inner Elbow

Purpose: Strike, press, hold, throw.

Typical use: Strike to back of head. Depending on technique, use tense or relaxed muscles, flexed or straight arm. Used for snapping strikes, clothesline strikes, holds, chokes, and takedowns. Often used against head targets or to trap a kicking leg.

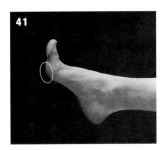

Ball Foot
Purpose: Strike.
Typical use: Front Ball Kick.
Formed by pointing instep, curling back toes, tensing area around toes and ankle. Used for kicks. Strike with padded area between arch and base of toes. Foot also formed as in #48 (used for Roundhouse Kick).

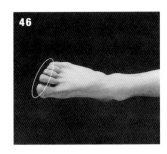

Cutting Foot
Purpose: Slashing or cutting.
Typical use: Cutting Crescent Kick.
Formed like a Knife Foot with toes uncurled. Used to cut or scratch sensitive targets such as eyes, ears nose, lips, and neck. Slash with tips and toenails of five toes, or with the hard front-edge of shoe sole.

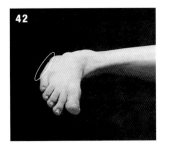

Knife Foot
Purpose: Strike, block, press, choke.
Typical use: Side Kick, pin knee.
Form in one of three ways: curl toes up (better ankle flexibility); curl toes down (easier to tighten foot); or curl big toe up and others down. Used for kicks, holds, chokes, takedowns, and pins. Strike with tensed outer edge.

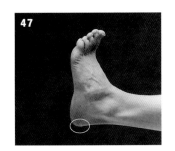

Back Heel
Purpose: Strike, throw.
Typical use: Spin Kick, Axe Kick.
Formed by retracting foot, curling toes upward, tensing ankle and foot. Foot bent about 90°. Used for power kicks to any target, or for reaping throws to lower leg. Strike with bony area below Achilles tendon.

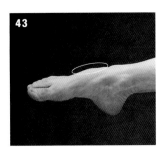

Instep Foot
Purpose: Strike.
Typical use: Roundhouse Kick.
Formed by pointing instep and toes, tensing ankle. Used for Roundhouse Kicks to knees, ribs, and head, or Front Instep Kicks to groin. Strike with the top of the foot, between ankle and toes (instep bone).

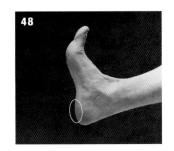

Inner Heel
Purpose: Strike.
Typical use: Shin Kick.
Formed by retracting foot, curling toes upward, tensing ankle and foot. Used for power or glancing strikes to any low target, such as kneecap or sensitive nerves on inner shin. Strike with bony area of inner heel.

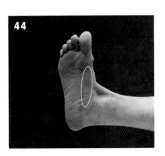

Arch Foot
Purpose: Strike, block, throw.
Typical use: Inside Crescent Kick.
Formed same as Knife Foot. Degree which foot is bent at ankle depends on technique. Used for kicks, blocks, foot sweeps, or pressing takedowns to back of knee. Strike with inside edge of foot between heel and ball.

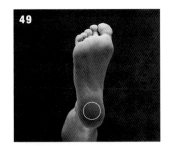

Bottom Heel
Purpose: Strike, press, hold, throw.
Typical use: Back Kick, Stamp Kick.
Formed by retracting foot, curling toes back, tensing ankle and bottom of foot. Used for a wide variety of kicks, stomps, holds, pins, and sacrifice throws. Contact area is base of heel bone.

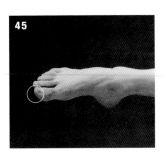

Spear Foot
Purpose: Strike, press.
Typical use: Front Toe Kick to armpit.
Formed by pointing instep with toes bunched tightly together. Used for pinpoint thrusting attacks to nerves or soft protected areas such as ribs, throat, or back of knee. Strike with the tip of big toe or point of shoe.

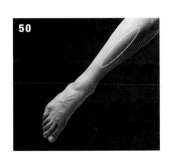

Front Lower Leg
Purpose: Strike, block, press, throw.
Typical use: Leg blocks, arm bar.
Formed by pointing instep and toes, tensing ankle and lower leg. Used for kicks to mid-section or legs, blocks against kicks, arm bars, chokes, pins, and leg-trap throws. Contact area is tibia bone at front of leg.

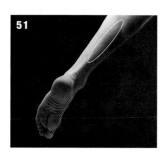

Back Lower Leg
Purpose: Hold, press, throw.
Typical use: Leg throws, pin.
Form by either extending or retracting foot based on technique. Used for holds, chokes, pins, and leg throws. Contact area is tensed muscles on the back of leg, from upper calf to Achilles tendon.

Shoulder and Upper arm
Purpose: Strike, block, hold, throw.
Typical use: Shoulder throw, butt.
Used for strikes, elbow breaks, butts, holds, pins, arm bars, throws, and takedowns. Butts are used to create space or setup a technique. Contact area and muscle tensing varies based upon technique executed.

Front Knee
Purpose: Strike, press, hold.
Typical use: Knee thrust to ribs.
Knee-flex and foot position varies depending upon technique. Used for strikes, thrusts, holds, chokes, and pins. Exercise extreme caution when using knee strikes, as area is very vulnerable to permanent damage.

Chest and Abdomen
Purpose: Strike, press, hold, throw.
Typical use: Chest butt, arm bar.
Used for butts, elbow breaks, arm bars, body pins, and throws. Contact area is upper chest or tensed abdominal muscles. Be careful not to compress diaphragm or shock sternum (heart), during butt strikes.

Back Knee
Purpose: Hold, throw.
Typical use: Foot-Plant Throw.
Knee-flex and foot position varies, depending upon technique. Used for holds, throws, takedowns, and ground fighting. Its use is explained in greater detail in the chapters outlining these techniques.

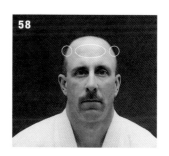

Forehead and Side of Head
Purpose: Strike, press.
Typical use: Light head butt to face.
Used for strikes and butts, pushing to maneuver when grappling, and pressing when pinning. Contact area is thickest part of skull at forehead or side. Use extreme caution as trauma to your brain is possible.

Upper Leg
Purpose: Hold, press, hold, throw.
Typical use: Leg throw, body pin.
Form by either extending or flexing knee, based on technique. Used for holds, arm bars, chokes, pins, and leg throws. Contact area is back or front of upper leg, depending upon specific technique being executed.

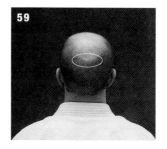

Back of Head
Purpose: Strike.
Typical use: Light head butt.
Use to hit up into underside of chin, or to strike face of attacker when held from behind. Contact area is thickest part of skull at back of head. Use extreme caution as trauma to your brain is possible.

Hip and Buttocks
Purpose: Strike, push, throw.
Typical use: Bear-hug escape.
Used for hip butts, holds, pins, hip throws, and takedowns. Often used to create space or set up a technique. Contact area is usually outer hip and buttocks, depending upon technique to be executed.

Chin
Purpose: Pressure on nerves.
Typical use: Naked Choke escape.
Used to press or gouge nerves when being held, and use of your hands and feet is restricted. Contact area is bony point of the chin, with jaw closed and teeth locked together (important or you will damage jaw).

The stances you will use depend upon the techniques you are executing, the martial art you are practicing, personal preference, and a variety of other factors. It is not possible to cover all of the stances used when executing striking techniques, as there are simply too many variables. Nonetheless, there are a few fundamental stances that are found in many practical or self-defense oriented martial arts. They are shown opposite. Generally speaking, it is better to think of stances as the links in a series of continuous movements, rather than as precisely defined foot placements. A rigid approach only limits your technique and your ability to adapt and improvise based on the constantly changing dynamics of combat. Most stances fall into two basic categories: relaxed stances and fighting stances.

Relaxed Stances

Relaxed stances resemble everyday standing or sitting postures. Since one never knows when they might be attacked, reacting and applying self-defense techniques from relaxed stances is an important skill for students to learn. Self-defense oriented martial arts, such as Hapkido, also make significant use of relaxed stances to camouflage tactics and lure an opponent into a false sense of security. Attacking and defending from relaxed stances is also useful when one wishes to maintain a low profile or minimize disturbance to people nearby.

Fighting Stances

In fighting stances, the position of the hands, feet, and body is optimized to facilitate execution of techniques. There are many types of fighting stances. The three shown at right are found in many practical martial arts. These stances can be used in a wide variety of circumstances to launch a broad range of techniques, such as strikes, kicks, holds, and throws. The Front Stance tends to be more offensive, whereas the Back Stance usually favors defense. The Side Stance is mostly used to set up specific kicks or spinning strikes, such as side kicks, back kicks, hook kicks, spin kicks, or turning hand-strikes.

1. Relaxed Standing Stance

Weight Distribution: Equal between both feet. This basic ready stance is often used to disguise tactics and intent. Place your feet shoulder-width apart with the knees slightly bent. Hands are open and hanging loosely at side. The entire body should be relaxed, ready to quickly respond. Do not adopt any hand or foot positions that could be construed as a preparation to attack. Face is expressionless. This stance is also called a *Natural Stance*.

2. Relaxed Walking Stance

Weight Distribution: Constantly changing. This posture is actually a form of offensive movement as well as a stance. It is used to disguise tactics and intent while being constantly mobile. Adopt a normal walk with relaxed arms and legs swinging freely and naturally. The flowing continuous movement of the hands, arms, and feet make this an excellent posture for launching disguised strikes, blocks, holds, or throws.

3. Front Stance

Weight Distribution: 50–60% front foot. This basic fighting stance is highly mobile, and good for fast footwork and entering. It is excellent for launching strikes, holds, or throws, but lacks stability if you are grappling at close range. Position the feet about 1 to 1.5 times your shoulder-width apart. The back foot may be flat or raised on the ball. This stance is commonly seen in a variety of styles, from boxing to Olympic Taekwondo.

4. Side Stance

Weight Distribution: Equal between both feet. This is a good stance for executing side kicks, back kicks, and turning kicks—or for fighting two opposing opponents 180° apart. This stance has poor lateral mobility, but is good for moving forward or backward. Position the feet about 1.5 times your shoulder-width, with the legs equally bent. Align the shoulders and hips with the feet. To face an opponent behind you, simply turn your head and shift the arms.

5. Back Stance

Weight Distribution: 50–75% back foot. This basic defensive stance possesses a good balance between stability and mobility. More weight on the back foot favors defense and use of the front leg for countering and blocking. Position the feet about 1.5 times your shoulder-width, with both legs bent. The front foot points straight forward, the rear foot points sideways (slightly less than 90°), the heels align. Shoulders and hips align with feet.

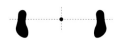

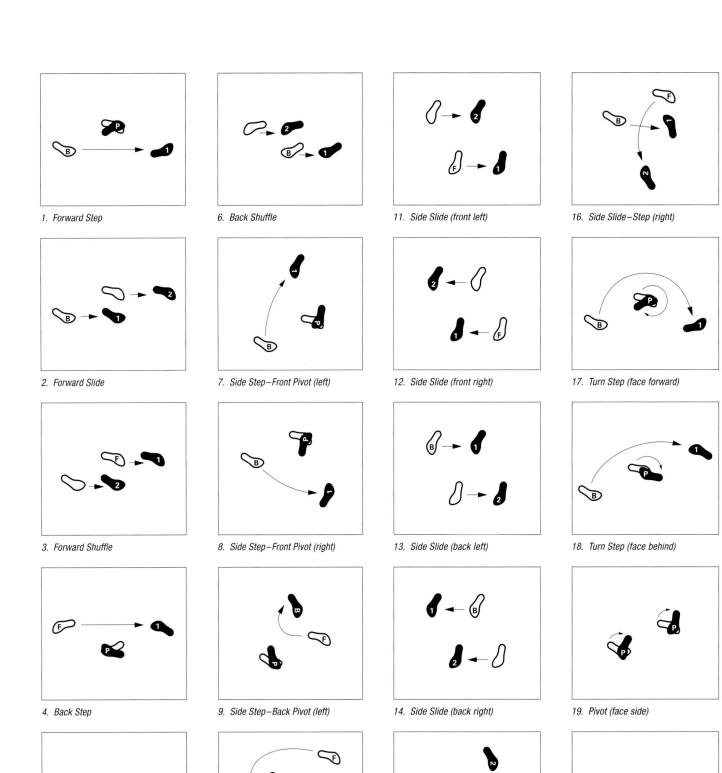

1. Forward Step

6. Back Shuffle

11. Side Slide (front left)

16. Side Slide–Step (right)

2. Forward Slide

7. Side Step–Front Pivot (left)

12. Side Slide (front right)

17. Turn Step (face forward)

3. Forward Shuffle

8. Side Step–Front Pivot (right)

13. Side Slide (back left)

18. Turn Step (face behind)

4. Back Step

9. Side Step–Back Pivot (left)

14. Side Slide (back right)

19. Pivot (face side)

5. Back Slide

10. Side Step–Back Pivot (right)

15. Side Slide–Step (left)

20. Pivot (face behind)

Most standing footwork derives from about 40 basic steps, which are combined or altered to create innumerable possibilities. During grappling, short steps with wider stances are usually preferred for stability and to prevent an opponent from sweeping your feet or throwing you. Steps 31–40 are variations modified for close-range grappling.

Outlined feet indicate start position; *solid* feet indicate ending. Numbers indicate which foot moves first.

P	Pivot
B	Back Foot
F	Front Foot
1, 2	Sequence

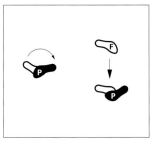

21. Step-Pivot (front step)

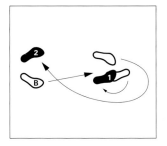

26. Rear Draw Turning

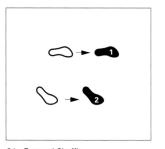

31. Forward Shuffle

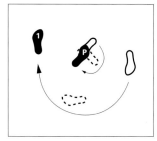

36. Forward Turn (right pivot)

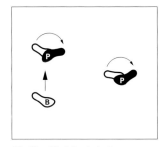

22. Step-Pivot (back step)

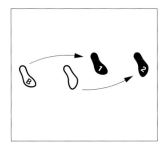

27. Cross Step Behind

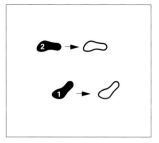

32. Back Shuffle

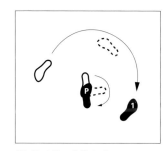

37. Back Turn (left pivot)

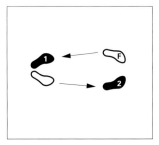

23. Front Draw

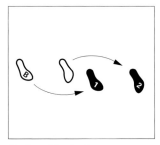

28. Cross Step Front

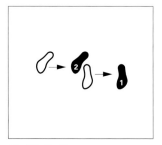

33. Side Shuffle

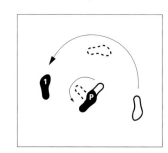

38. Back Turn (right pivot)

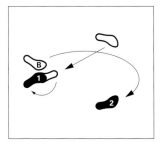

24. Front Draw Turning

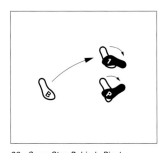

29. Cross Step Behind–Pivot

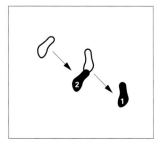

34. Diagonal Shuffle

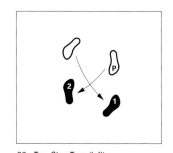

39. Two Step Turn (left)

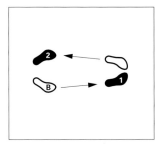

25. Rear Draw

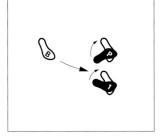

30. Cross Step Front–Pivot

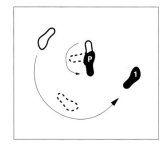

35. Forward Turn (left pivot)

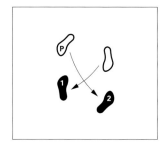

40. Two Step Turn (right)

Breakfalls

A *breakfall* is a specific method of falling, designed to protect your body from damage as you hit the ground. This involves specific formations of your body that minimize impact by dispersing force over a large surface area. Breakfall skills are commonly learned in conjunction with holds and throws, but can easily become necessary during any form of combat. When executing strikes, you may lose your balance and fall, get knocked over, or your punch or kick might be grabbed, leading to a throw. Breaking an arm or dislocating a shoulder can easily be avoided if you know how to fall. Four basic types of breakfalls, common to many martial arts, are shown at right. Additional breakfalls and more information can be found in the author's books *The Art of Throwing* and *The Art of Holding*.

Breakfalls should be learned from a qualified instructor to avoid injuries. The breakfall you will use is based on how you are thrown. In all breakfalls, you will attempt to control your body position while airborne. As your body lands in the proper position, you will usually *slap* and emit an *energy-shout* at the same time. In some martial arts, an energy-shout is not used and practitioners will instead either exhale or hold their breath.

The Slap

In most breakfalls you will slap with your hand and forearm, or entire arm, to distribute the force of impact. This also helps to position your body and assists in timing. The force of your slap must be adjusted based on the hardness of the surface you are falling onto. While it is common to see students endlessly practicing forceful slaps on the mat, these same slaps will cause you to injure or break your hand when falling on hard surfaces like concrete. In some soft-style martial arts, the slap is barely articulated or nonexistent, since the focus is on blending with the ground.

The Energy-Shout

An energy-shout is an abrupt shout designed to focus your energy and power, and was covered previously in this chapter, under

Energetic Concepts. During breakfalls, an energy-shout helps protect the body from injury, keeps the wind from being knocked out of your lungs, and causes your body to naturally relax on impact. Some martial arts do not use a shout, but instead focus on relaxing and blending with the ground. In some Chinese arts, practitioners are taught to tense their body and hold their breath during a breakfall, the idea being that this prevents organ damage from the force of impact.

1. Front Fall

As you fall forward, position your hands in front of your face, with your bent-arms at a 45° angle, hands aligned with forearms. While airborne, spread your feet shoulder-width apart or wider. As you approach the ground, slap downward with both hands and forearms, as you shout or exhale. Your hands should make contact slightly before your forearms. The underside of your toes should make contact at the same time.

As you fall, turn your head sideways to avoid accidentally breaking your nose. Do not allow your knees or torso to hit the ground. Try to absorb some of the shock by flexing your elbows and shoulders as you land. *Do not* land directly on the elbows (fracture), or reach out with your palms (broken wrist). When first learning to fall, practice from a kneeling position, progressing to squatting, then standing, and eventually airborne.

2. Back Fall

As you fall backward, cross your arms and tuck your chin against your chest, to keep your head from hitting the ground. As you land on the back of your shoulders, slap the ground with both hands and arms at a 45° angle from your body, and shout or exhale. Quickly retract your hands to prepare for your next technique. When falling from a standing posture (see photos), keep your hips close to your heels.

Do not slap higher than 45°. It is ineffective, and will often stress the shoulders, or cause the wind to be knocked out of you. Keep your back curved as you fall. When first learning,

progress from lying to sitting, to squatting, to standing, then airborne. Try to avoid landing on the middle or lower back, since this stresses the spine. High falls can be difficult, since minor errors often result in neck injuries.

4. Sit-Out Side Fall

This breakfall is used when you are falling to your side or rear-corner. As one leg is swept or reaped, you will lower yourself using your supporting leg. Sit back toward your rear-corner, rolling onto your side, as you slap the ground with one arm at a 45° angle from your body, and shout or exhale. Allow the rolling motion to carry your legs upward. The slap is often not needed, but helps time your actions.

This is a very low-impact fall, since you are controlling your own descent throughout. It sometimes helps to think of it as a back roll executed on the side of your body. Keep your buttock close to your heel as you sit back. This breakfall is often confused with the next technique, however, they are quite different. In this breakfall, one leg supports your fall. In the *Sweep Side Fall,* both feet leave the ground.

4. Sweep Side Fall

This breakfall is used when one or both legs are swept out from under you. You will land on the side of your body, as you slap the ground with one arm (at a 45° angle from the body) and shout or exhale. The entire right side of your body and your left foot contact the ground at the same time. The left leg is bent and vertical, landing on the ball of the foot. The right leg is slightly bent, with the sole turned upward to protect the ankle.

Make sure you tuck your chin, turn your right foot upward to protect your protruding ankle from hitting the ground, and land on the back of your right shoulder—not the side, or serious injury will result. When compared to the previous *Sit-Out Side Fall,* this fall involves greater impact, with both legs contacting the ground. The force of the throw will not allow you to *sit-out* as described in the previous breakfall. This fall may be needed when you cannot land properly after high jump kicks.

1. Front Fall

2. Back Fall

3. Sit-Out Side Fall

4. Sweep Side Fall

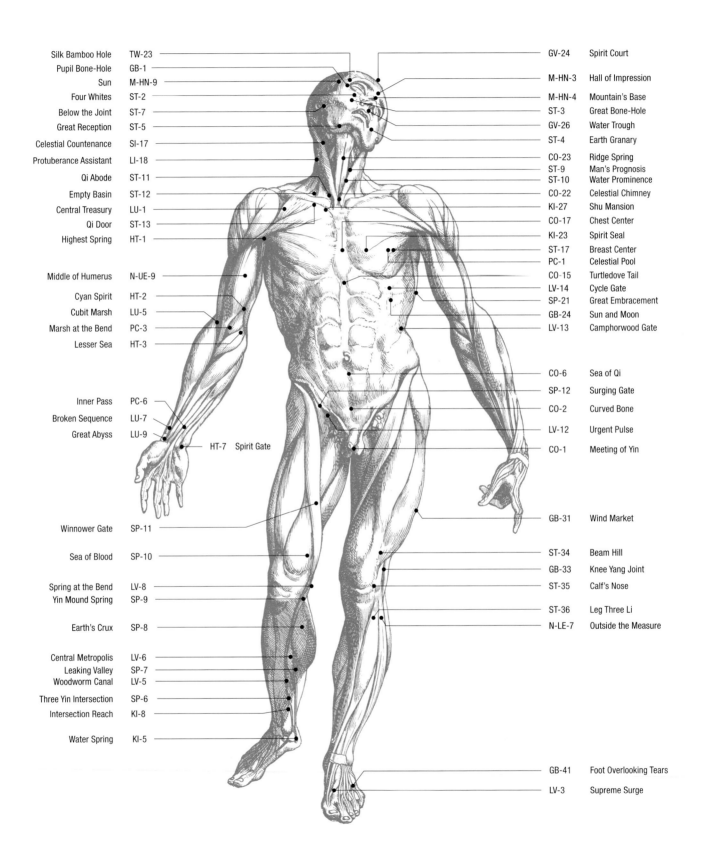

Silk Bamboo Hole	TW-23		GV-24	Spirit Court
Pupil Bone-Hole	GB-1		M-HN-3	Hall of Impression
Sun	M-HN-9		M-HN-4	Mountain's Base
Four Whites	ST-2		ST-3	Great Bone-Hole
Below the Joint	ST-7		GV-26	Water Trough
Great Reception	ST-5		ST-4	Earth Granary
Celestial Countenance	SI-17		CO-23	Ridge Spring
Protuberance Assistant	LI-18		ST-9	Man's Prognosis
Qi Abode	ST-11		ST-10	Water Prominence
Empty Basin	ST-12		CO-22	Celestial Chimney
Central Treasury	LU-1		KI-27	Shu Mansion
Qi Door	ST-13		CO-17	Chest Center
Highest Spring	HT-1		KI-23	Spirit Seal
			ST-17	Breast Center
			PC-1	Celestial Pool
Middle of Humerus	N-UE-9		CO-15	Turtledove Tail
Cyan Spirit	HT-2		LV-14	Cycle Gate
Cubit Marsh	LU-5		SP-21	Great Embracement
Marsh at the Bend	PC-3		GB-24	Sun and Moon
Lesser Sea	HT-3		LV-13	Camphorwood Gate
			CO-6	Sea of Qi
Inner Pass	PC-6		SP-12	Surging Gate
Broken Sequence	LU-7		CO-2	Curved Bone
Great Abyss	LU-9		LV-12	Urgent Pulse
	HT-7	Spirit Gate	CO-1	Meeting of Yin
Winnower Gate	SP-11		GB-31	Wind Market
Sea of Blood	SP-10		ST-34	Beam Hill
			GB-33	Knee Yang Joint
Spring at the Bend	LV-8		ST-35	Calf's Nose
Yin Mound Spring	SP-9		ST-36	Leg Three Li
Earth's Crux	SP-8		N-LE-7	Outside the Measure
Central Metropolis	LV-6			
Leaking Valley	SP-7			
Woodworm Canal	LV-5			
Three Yin Intersection	SP-6			
Intersection Reach	KI-8			
Water Spring	KI-5			
			GB-41	Foot Overlooking Tears
			LV-3	Supreme Surge

The illustrations on these pages show 106 common pressure point targets used in the martial arts. Each point is labeled using both its alphanumeric symbol, and the English translation of the point's Chinese name. Korean and Japanese translations are usually similar, if not identical. *Essential Anatomy for Healing and Martial Arts*, by the same author, contains additional pressure point targets and charts, a detailed discussion of pressure point fighting principles, a comprehensive presentation of human anatomy in both Eastern and Western medical systems, and an index listing the precise anatomical location of more than 380 pressure points, cross-referenced to nerves, blood vessels, and other anatomical landmarks.

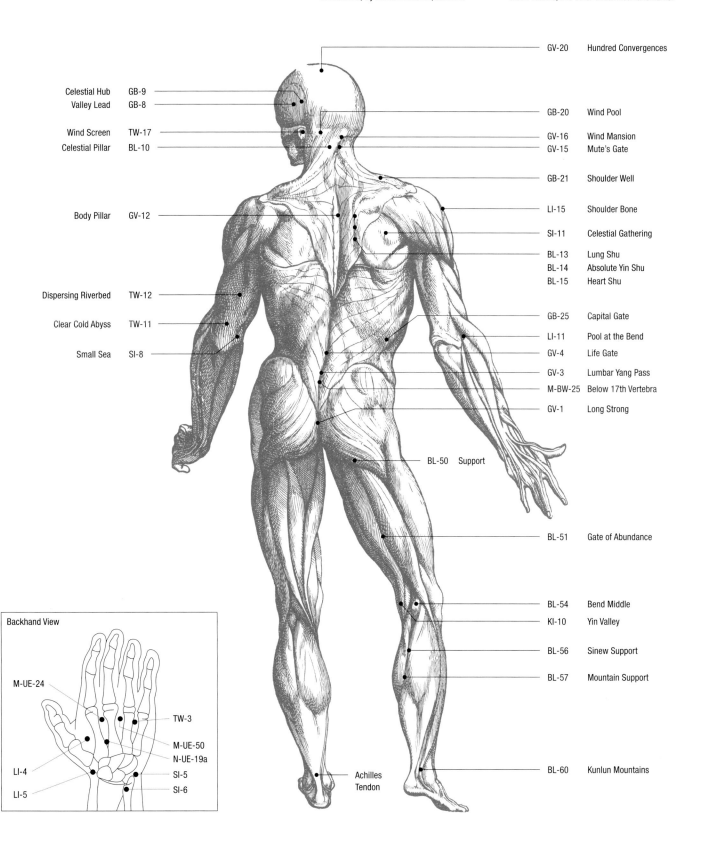

Celestial Hub — GB-9
Valley Lead — GB-8
Wind Screen — TW-17
Celestial Pillar — BL-10
Body Pillar — GV-12
Dispersing Riverbed — TW-12
Clear Cold Abyss — TW-11
Small Sea — SI-8

GV-20 — Hundred Convergences
GB-20 — Wind Pool
GV-16 — Wind Mansion
GV-15 — Mute's Gate
GB-21 — Shoulder Well
LI-15 — Shoulder Bone
SI-11 — Celestial Gathering
BL-13 — Lung Shu
BL-14 — Absolute Yin Shu
BL-15 — Heart Shu
GB-25 — Capital Gate
LI-11 — Pool at the Bend
GV-4 — Life Gate
GV-3 — Lumbar Yang Pass
M-BW-25 — Below 17th Vertebra
GV-1 — Long Strong
BL-50 — Support
BL-51 — Gate of Abundance
BL-54 — Bend Middle
KI-10 — Yin Valley
BL-56 — Sinew Support
BL-57 — Mountain Support
BL-60 — Kunlun Mountains
Achilles Tendon

Backhand View
M-UE-24
TW-3
M-UE-50
N-UE-19a
SI-5
SI-6
LI-4
LI-5

BL-10	Back of neck, 1.3 units lateral to GV-15, within hairline, on lateral side of trapezius muscle.
BL-13	Upper back, 1.5 units lateral to lower edge of spinous process of 3rd thoracic vertebra.
BL-14	Upper back, 1.5 units lateral to lower edge of spinous process of 4th thoracic vertebra.
BL-15	Upper back, 1.5 units lateral to lower edge of spinous process of 5th thoracic vertebra.
BL-50	Buttock, at midpoint of crease below buttock (transverse gluteal crease).
BL-51	Back of thigh, 6 units below BL-50 on line joining BL-50 to BL-54.
BL-54	Back of knee, midpoint of transverse crease, between biceps + semitendinosus m. tendons.
BL-56	Lower leg, 3 units above BL-57, in center of belly of gastrocnemius m. (calf).
BL-57	Lower leg, directly below belly of gastrocnemius muscle, on line joining BL-54 to Achilles tendon.
BL-60	Outer ankle, recess halfway between protruding bone at ankle and Achilles tendon, level with tip.
CO-1	In center of perineum, between anus and genitals.
CO-2	Front midline, directly above pubic bone (pubic symphysis), 5 units below navel, (pulse is felt).
CO-6	Front midline of abdomen, 1.5 units below navel.
CO-15	Front midline, 7 units above navel, usually below xiphoid process (depends on length of cartilage).
CO-17	Front midline of chest, level with 4th intercostal space, level and between nipples, on sternum.
CO-22	Front midline, at center of sternal notch (top edge of sternum, at base of throat).
CO-23	Front midline of throat, above Adam's apple, in recess at upper edge of hyoid bone.
GB-1	About 0.5 unit lateral to outer corner of eye, in recess on lateral side of orbit (bony eye socket).
GB-8	Side of head, above apex of ear, in recess 1.5 units within hairline (point is felt when biting).
GB-9	Side of head, above and behind ear, 2 units within hairline, about 0.5 unit behind GB-8.
GB-20	Back of neck, below occipital bone, in recess between sternoceidomastoid m. and trapezius m.
GB-21	Shoulder, halfway between C7 vertebra and protruding bone at top of shoulder (acromion).
GB-24	Below nipple, between cartilage of 7th+8th ribs, one rib space below and slightly lateral to LV-14.

GB-25	Side of trunk, at lower edge of floating end of 12th rib (lowest rib).
GB-31	Outer thigh, 7 units above kneecap, at end of middle finger when arm hangs at side.
GB-33	Outer thigh, in recess above bony knob of femur, between bone and biceps femoris tendon.*
GB-41	Top of foot, in recess distal and between junction of 4th and 5th metatarsal bones.
GV-1	Halfway between tip of tailbone (coccyx) and anus.
GV-3	Midline of back, below spinous process of 4th lumbar vertebra.
GV-4	Midline of back, below spinous process of 2nd lumbar vertebra.
GV-12	Midline of back, below spinous process of 3rd thoracic vertebra.
GV-15	Back midline of neck, in recess 0.5 unit below GV-16, 0.5 unit within hairline.
GV-16	Midline of neck, in recess below ext. occipital protuberance, at trapezius muscle attachments.
GV-20	Midline of head, 7 units above rear hairline, on midpoint of line joining earlobes and ear apexes.
GV-24	Midline, on top of head, 0.5 unit within front hairline.
GV-26	Front midline, in center of groove below nose (philtrum), slightly above midpoint.
HT-1	With arm raised, in center of axilla (armpit), on medial side of axillary artery.
HT-2	3 units above medial end of elbow crease and HT-3, in groove medial to biceps muscle.
HT-3	With elbow bent, at medial end of elbow crease, in recess anterior to protruding bone at elbow.
HT-7	On transverse wrist crease, in recess between ulna and pisiform bones, radial side of tendon.
KI-5	Inner heel, in recess above and in front of bulge in heel bone, 1 unit below level of ankle.
KI-8	Inner lower leg, 2 units above level of protruding bone at ankle, posterior to medial edge of tibia.
KI-10	Medial side of back of knee, between semitendinosus + semimembranosus tendons, level BL-54.
KI-23	Chest, in 4th intercostal space (between ribs), 2 units lateral to body midline, level with nipple.
KI-27	Chest, in recess at lower edge of medial head of clavicle, 2 units lateral to body midline.
LI-4	Center of muscle between 1st + 2nd metacarpals on back of hand (web of thumb), slightly to 2nd.

LI-5	Radial side of wrist, in recess between extensor muscle tendons at base of thumb.
LI-11	In recess at lateral end of elbow crease, midway between LU-5 and protruding humerus bone.
LI-15	With arm raised, in a recess at edge of shoulder joint, slightly forward to middle of deltoid muscle.
LI-18	Side of neck, level with Adam's apple tip, directly below ear, on rear part of sternoceidomastoid m.
LU-1	Chest, 1 unit below lateral end of clavicle, in first intercostal space, 6 units lateral midline (pulse).
LU-5	Crease of elbow, at radial side of biceps tendon, at origin of brachioradialis muscle.
LU-7	Thumb-side of forearm, in crevice at lateral edge of radius bone, 1.5 units above wrist crease.
LU-9	Wrist at transverse crease, in recess on radial side of radial artery, where pulse is felt.
LV-3	Top of foot, in recess distal and between junction of 1st and 2nd metatarsal bones (above web).
LV-5	5 units above tip of protruding bone at inner ankle, between posterior edge of tibia and calf m.
LV-6	Inner ankle, 7 units above tip of protruding bone at inner ankle, on posterior edge of tibia.
LV-8	Inner knee joint. When bent, point is at medial end of crease, above tendons attaching at joint.
LV-12	Inguinal groove, 2.5 units lateral to midline, lateral to pubic symphysis, 5 units below navel.
LV-13	Trunk, below free end of 11th floating rib, 2 units above level of navel, 6 units lateral to midline.
LV-14	Chest, near medial end of 6th intercostal space (between ribs), 2 ribs below nipple.
M-BW-25	Back midline, 1 vertebra below GV-3, at lumbosacral joint (5th lumbar and 1st sacral vertebras).
M-HN-3	Front midline, in recess halfway between medial ends of eyebrows (glabella), also called GV-24.5.
M-HN-4	Front midline, lowest point on bridge of nose, halfway between inner canthi of left + right eyes.
M-HN-9	Temple, in recess 1 unit posterior to the midpoint between outer canthus of eye and tip of eyebrow.
M-UE-24	Back of hand, between 2nd and 3rd metacarpal bones, 0.5 unit proximal to base joints of fingers.
M-UE-50	Back of hand, between 3rd and 4th metacarpal bones, 0.5 unit proximal to base joints of fingers.
N-LE-7	Outer lower leg below knee, 1 unit lateral to ST-36.
N-UE-9	Front upper arm, in center of biceps brachii muscle, 4.5 units below axillary (armpit) fold.

N-UE-19a	Back of hand, at forked recess where 2nd and 3rd metacarpal bones merge.
PC-1	Chest, 1 unit lateral to nipple, in 4th intercostal space.
PC-3	Inner elbow, on transverse crease, slightly medial to tendon of biceps brachii muscle.
PC-6	Forearm, 2 units above wrist crease, between tendons of long palmar m. and radial flexor m.
SI-5	Ulnar side of wrist, in recess between ulna bone and triquetral bone (wrist joint).
SI-6	With palm facing chest, 0.5 unit proximal wrist, in bony recess on radial side of head of ulna bone.
SI-8	In recess on flat spot between elbow point (ulna) and medial bony knob of humerus (arm flexed).
SI-11	Flat part of scapula, halfway between left + right edges, 1/3 the distance between ridge and base.
SI-17	Directly behind corner of jaw (angle of mandible), recess at anterior edge of sternocleidomastoid m.
SP-6	3 units above protruding bone at inner ankle, on rear (posterior) edge of tibia.
SP-7	6 units above protruding bone at inner ankle, 3 units above SP-6.
SP-8	3 units below protruding tibia bone at inner knee, on line joining SP-9 and protruding anklebone.
SP-9	In recess below protruding tibia at inner knee, between rear edge of tibia and gastrocnemius m.
SP-10	Thigh, 2 units above top medial edge of kneecap, on medial edge of vastus medialis m. (on bulge).
SP-11	Thigh, 6 units above SP-10, at medial side of sartorius m., between SP-10 + 12 (pulse is felt).
SP-12	In inguinal crease, lateral side of femoral artery, 3.5 units lateral to CO-2, where pulse is felt.
SP-21	Trunk, on midaxillary line, 6 units below armpit, halfway between armpit and free end of 11th rib.
ST-2	In a recess on top edge of cheekbone, aligned with eye pupil.
ST-3	Directly below eye pupil and ST-2, level with lower edge of nostril.
ST-4	Slightly lateral to corner of mouth, directly below ST-3, a faint pulse is felt close below.
ST-5	In a groove-like recess along bottom of jaw bone, on front edge of masseter muscle (pulse is felt).
ST-7	In front of ear, in recess at lower edge of zygomatic arch, forward of jaw joint.
ST-9	Side of neck, level with Adam's apple tip, at front edge of sternocleidomastoid m., along carotid a.
ST-10	On front edge of sternocleidomastoid muscle, halfway between ST-9 and ST-11.
ST-11	Front base of neck, in recess between two heads of sternocleidomastoid m., at end of clavicle.
ST-12	In a recess at top edge of middle of clavicle, aligned with nipple, 4 units lateral to midline.
ST-13	In a recess at lower edge of middle of clavicle, above and aligned with nipple.
ST-17	Chest, in center of nipple. This acupoint is often used as a landmark to locate other acupoints.
ST-34	Thigh, 2 units above top lateral edge of kneecap, between rectus femoris and vastus lateralis m.
ST-35	In a recess below kneecap, lateral to patellar ligament when knee is bent.
ST-36	Lower leg, 3 units below ST-35, about 1 unit lateral to crest of tibia bone (shinbone).
TW-3	Back of hand, between 4th and 5th metacarpal bones, in recess proximal base joints of fingers.
TW-11	Back of upper arm, 2 units above point of elbow, on triceps brachii tendon.
TW-12	Back of upper arm, at end of lateral head of triceps brachii muscle.
TW-17	In recess behind ear lobe, between mastoid process (on skull) and jawbone (mandible).
TW-23	Side of head, in recess at lateral end of eyebrow.

Locating Pressure Points

Pressure points (also called *acupoints*) are usually located in depressions at bones, joints, and muscles. The area affecting each point is usually the size of a dime, but can be as small as a pin head. Some points are easy to locate by simply probing around, since they are very sensitive to pressure. Others are well hidden and require very precise targeting. The angle of attack is often critical. Feel for a slight depression or hollow at each point. This might be a perceived as a slight depression in the bone, or a small space between muscle fibers, tendons, and muscles.

Location Methods

In ancient China, a system using body landmarks and a relative unit of measurement called a *cun*, assisted practitioners in locating points. This system is still in use today. A cun (also called a body inch, unit, or finger unit) varies in length based on the proportion and size of the individual being measured. The length or width of different parts of the fingers are used to make rough estimates of point locations, as shown at right.

Terms Used in This Reference

When describing the locations of pressure points on the human body, it is necessary to use precise anatomical terms to avoid confusion. For example, "above the wrist joint" can refer to either side of the wrist, depending on how the arm is oriented (raised, lowered); whereas, "proximal" is precise, regardless of orientation.

Superior:	Toward the head or upper part of a structure.
Inferior:	Away from head, or toward lower part of a structure.
Anterior:	Nearer to, or at the front of body.
Posterior:	Nearer to, or at the back of body.
Medial:	Nearer to the midline of body, or a structure.
Lateral:	Farther from the midline of body, or a structure.
Proximal:	Nearer to the attachment of an extremity, to trunk or a structure.
Distal:	Farther from the attachment of an extremity, to trunk or a structure.
Superficial:	Toward or on the surface of body.
Deep:	Away from the surface of body
Unit:	Relative unit of measurement based on use of the fingers.

Abbreviations: (m.) muscle, (n.) nerve, (a.) artery, (v.) vein

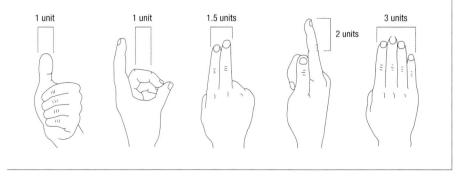

1 unit   1 unit   1.5 units   2 units   3 units

STRIKE SUMMARY

	Arm Strikes	Leg Strikes

This book outlines 421 basic striking techniques used in martial arts. They are summarized at right and shown in subsequent chapters. Basic striking techniques are organized as follows:

Arm Strikes

50 Hand Strikes
9 Lower Arm Strikes
8 Elbow Strikes

Leg Strikes

31 Standing Kicks
4 Knee Strikes
37 Ground Kicks
14 Jump Kicks

Head + Body Strikes

6 Head Strikes
4 Body Strikes

Combinations

61 Arm Strike Combinations
56 Kick Combinations
26 Mixed Combinations

Avoiding + Blocking

7 Avoiding Techniques
50 Blocking Techniques

Defense Against Punches

34 Counters Using Strikes

Defense Against Kicks

16 Counters Using Strikes

Defense Against Holds

8 Counters Using Strikes

Technique names are based on commonly used terms. However, within the martial arts there still remains a great deal of variability in term use. Many different terms are often used to represent the same technique. Whenever possible, the clearest or most widely accepted nomenclature is used.

Hand Strikes

1 Jab Punch
2 Straight Punch
3 Vertical Punch
4 Overhead Punch
5 Hook Punch
6 Uppercut Punch
7 Back Punch
8 Rising Punch
9 Outside Back Fist
10 Descending Back Fist
11 Rising Back Fist
12 Raking Back Fist
13 Outside Hammer Fist
14 Descending Hammer Fist
15 Inside Hammer Fist
16 Twin Hammer Fist
17 Outside Thumb Fist
18 Inside Thumb Fist
19 Rising Thumb Fist
20 Twin Thumb Fist
21 Middle Finger Fist
22 Index Finger Fist
23 Knuckle Fist
24 Knuckle Hand
25 Outside Knife Hand
26 Inside Knife Hand
27 Descending Knife Hand
28 Cutting Hand
29 Spear Hand
30 Spear Hand–2 Fingers
31 Spear Hand–2 Spread
32 Spear Hand–1 Finger
33 Straight Back Hand
34 Circular Back Hand
35 Ridge Hand
36 Ox Jaw Hand
37 Chicken Hand

38 Tiger Mouth Hand
39 Straight Palm Heel
40 Descending Palm Heel
41 Uppercut Palm Heel
42 Hook Palm Heel
43 Inside Palm Heel
44 Open Hand
45 Bear Hand
46 Claw Hand
47 Five Fingertip Hand
48 Thumb Hand
49 Pincer Hand
50 Eagle Hand

Lower Arm Strikes

1 Straight Bent Wrist
2 Outside Bent Wrist
3 Inside Bent Wrist
4 Rising Bent Wrist
5 Inner Wrist
6 Outer Wrist
7 Outer Forearm
8 Inner Forearm
9 Hook Forearm

Elbow Strikes

1 Rising Elbow
2 Descending Elbow
3 Inside Elbow
4 Outside Elbow
5 Assisted Inside Elbow
6 Assisted Side Elbow
7 Back Elbow
8 Inner Elbow

Standing Kicks

1 Front Ball Kick
2 Front Heel Kick
3 Front Thrust Kick
4 Rising Front Kick
5 Roundhouse Kick
6 45° Roundhouse Kick
7 Shin Roundhouse Kick
8 Reverse Roundhouse Kick
9 Side Thrust Kick
10 Side Snap Kick
11 Rising Side Kick
12 Push Kick
13 Back Kick
14 Back Side Kick
15 Uppercut Back Kick
16 Rising Back Kick
17 Rising Heel Kick
18 Stamp Kick
19 Descending Arch Kick
20 Shin Kick
21 Circular Inner-Heel Kick
22 Inside Hook Kick
23 Circular Blade Kick
24 Reverse Circular Blade Kick
25 Inside Crescent Kick
26 Outside Crescent Kick
27 Outside Axe Kick
28 Inside Axe Kick
29 Hook Kick
30 Spin Kick
31 Hook Spin Kick

Knee Strikes

1 Rising Knee Strike
2 Front Knee Strike
3 Roundhouse Knee Strike
4 Side Knee Strike

Ground Kicks

1 Drop Front Kick
2 Drop Roundhouse Kick
3 Drop Side Kick
4 Drop Back Kick
5 Drop Axe Kick
6 Drop Hook Kick
7 Drop Spin Kick
8 Drop Twin Front Kick
9 Drop Twin Roundhouse Kick
10 Drop Twin Side Kick
11 Drop Twin Back Kick
12 Drop Twin Overhead Kick
13 Drop Front Split Kick
14 Drop Side Split Kick
15 Drop Overhead Split Kick
16 Seated Front Kick
17 Seated Front Blade Kick
18 Seated Front Toe Kick
19 Seated Roundhouse Kick
20 Seated Reverse Roundhouse Kick
21 Seated Side Kick
22 Seated Back Kick
23 Seated Stamp Kick
24 Seated Circular Inner-Heel Kick
25 Seated Inside Crescent Kick
26 Seated Outside Crescent Kick
27 Seated Cutting Crescent Kick
28 Seated Axe Kick
29 Seated Inside Hook Kick
30 Seated Hook Kick
31 Seated Twin Front Kick
32 Seated Twin Roundhouse Kick
33 Seated Twin Side Kick
34 Seated Twin Overhead Kick
35 Seated Front Split Kick
36 Seated Side Split Kick
37 Seated Overhead Split Kick

Jump Kicks

1 Jump Front Kick
2 Jump Roundhouse Kick
3 Jump Side Kick
4 Jump Back Kick
5 Jump Turning Back Kick
6 Jump Axe Kick
7 Jump Hook Kick
8 Jump Spin Kick
9 Twin Front Kick
10 Twin Roundhouse Kick
11 Twin Side Kick
12 Twin Back Kick
13 Twin Front Split Kick
14 Twin Side Split Kick

Head + Body Strikes

1 Forehead Butt
2 Side Head Butt
3 Back Head Butt
4 Head Thrust
5 Chin Press
6 Biting
7 Shoulder Butt
8 Chest Butt
9 Side Hip Butt (hip)
10 Back Hip Butt (buttocks)

Combinations

There are innumerable possibilities for linking strikes together, for offensive or defensive purposes. A later chapter outlines 143 typical combination strikes.

Avoiding + Blocking

Fifty-seven typical techniques for neutralizing arm strikes and kicks are covered in a later chapter, organized as follows:

7 Avoiding Techniques
14 Soft Blocks
14 Hard Blocks
6 Shielding Blocks
16 Blocks Against Kicks

Defense Against Punches

Typical counterstriking techniques are covered in a later chapter, organized as follows:

20 Block + Strike
8 Block + Kick
6 Avoid + Strike

Defense Against Kicks

Sixteen typical counterstriking techniques are covered in a later chapter.

Defense Against Holds

Eight typical striking techniques used to counter simple holds and chokes are covered in a later chapter.

Arm strikes are hitting techniques that use specific surfaces of the hand, forearm, or elbow for delivering blows anywhere on the body. Arm strikes can be executed while standing, jumping, flying through the air, falling, kneeling, or reclining on the ground. Some martial arts possess hundreds of different arm strikes, used in a wide range of situations, while others use a more limited repertoire, often restricted to very specific circumstances. Knowing many strikes does not necessarily imply superiority in combat, but it does allow

ARM STRIKES

you to respond to a broader range of combative situations, and to better understand the strengths and limitations of strikes being directed against you. This chapter outlines 67 arm strikes used in Hapkido, which are also found in other martial art styles. The following pages will provide an overview of basic principles and a description of each arm strike, outlining their basic biomechanical qualities, appropriate uses, and relationships to each other. Typical self-defense applications can be found in subsequent chapters.

This chapter begins by outlining 50 basic hand strike techniques, which can be varied in innumerable ways depending upon need. Hand strikes are applied in four ways:

Single Strike – A single strike using one hand.

Alternate Hand Strikes – Multiple strikes in rapid sequence using alternating hands.

Consecutive Hand Strikes – Multiple strikes in rapid sequence using the same hand.

Twin Strikes – Striking with both hands at the same time. Impact is simultaneous, either to the same or to two different targets. Since both hands are attacking (no hands guarding), your own targets are extremely vulnerable to counterstrikes during the technique. For this reason, twin strikes are usually only used close in, as a surprise first-strike, or when the opponent's hands are otherwise occupied (e.g., choking you).

FORE FIST STRIKES

The Fore Fist, a clenched fist striking with the first two knuckles, is one of the most common hand formations used in striking. Fore Fist strikes, commonly called punches, can be executed from numerous positions to targets anywhere on the body. The method by which the Fore Fist is formed is very important and was covered under *Attack Points*. Contact area is usually the first two knuckles, although the smaller knuckles can also be used when pressing or punching lightly to pressure points. There are eight basic strikes

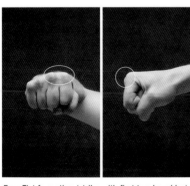

Fore Fist formation (strike with first two knuckles)

using the Fore Fist. They are outlined on the next five pages. Many of these strikes may also be used with other hand formations, such as the Thumb Fist, Middle Finger Fist, Index Finger Fist, Knuckle Fist, and Palm Heel.

Punching Fundamentals

In all Fore Fist strikes, punching power is generated by use of the entire body. This involves coordinated movement of the arms, shoulders, hips, and legs—all working together as a single unit supporting the punch. Power ideally begins in the hips and legs and is transmitted sequentially to the chest, shoulder, arm, and hand. The amount of leg thrust, hip turn, shoulder turn, and fist rotation varies based on the type of punch, stance you are punching from, use of lead or rear hand, and individual preference. When executing punches in rapid sequence, or when recovery speed is crucial, supporting body movements may become more abbreviated. When preparation for subsequent techniques is not essential and power is important, body movements may become more pronounced. Keep the arm and shoulder muscles relaxed until the last moment, or your punch will be slow, stiff, and ineffectual.

Use of the Arms

The speed and power of a punch is assisted by retracting the opposite arm during the strike. This is also necessary to prepare for the next blow, or to block a counterstrike thrown as you punch. The movement of the retracting hand mirrors the movements of the punching hand. When the punch is fully extended, the opposite hand is fully retracted. The timing of both arms is important to achieve proper balance between the two opposing muscle groups. You will find that punching speed and power increases as you increase the speed of the retracting hand.

The opposing arm motions used in punching may be launched from various positions, such as the hips, side of the torso, front of the shoulder, or directly from a guard position. The difference between traditional and modern punching forms are shown at right.

Traditional Punching Form

Historically, most martial arts executed punches from deep rooted stances, with the hands striking and retracting from the side of the torso or hips. For the warrior, a punch was often called upon to penetrate wooden armor, or to immobilize or kill an opponent as quickly as possible (one blow) in order to face other opponents in battle. Consequently, power was extremely important. Arguably, this still remains the most powerful punching position. However, as hand-to-hand fighting evolved in the latter twentieth century, retracting the hands to the torso became too slow and vulnerable, particularly when defending against counterstrikes to the head.

Modern Punching Form

Today, the hands are positioned higher and out in front, where they are more useful for quick blocks, strikes, and counters. It is still common to momentarily drop the punching hand to the torso or hip when executing powerful finishing punches, long hooks, or uppercuts. This is safer when the opponent is stunned and the risk of a counterstrike is unlikely. Withdrawing the hand to the hip is also used when pulling an opponent into a strike, by grabbing the arm. In this situation, the withdrawing hand often grasps specific pressure points, to activate other points your opposite arm will be striking. When defending from relaxed stances where deception is important, the first punch is commonly thrown from the hip, before adopting a guard.

Live-Hand Use

Historically, Hapkido single punches were often executed using a Live-Hand formation for the retracting arm. The Live-Hand was used to increase a strike's speed and power by increasing the flow of Ki. This technique is only practical with single strikes, finishing blows, or certain combinations (e.g., Live-Hand leads, rear hand delivers second strike), in which the Live-Hand does not need to be immediately reformed into a different hand formation. Live-Hand use becomes much more practical during elbow strikes, or punch-and-elbow strike combinations.

Basic punch with retracting arm (degree of fist rotation at impact can be varied to suit target characteristics or individual preference)

Punching from traditional low-hand position (Jab, Straight Punch)

Punching from modern high-hand position (Jab, Straight Punch)

Punching with a Live-Hand retracting arm (Straight Punch, Rising Elbow Strike)

1. Jab Punch

The Jab Punch is a fast, straight strike by the front hand, which is quickly retracted after impact. Jabs are executed while stationary or as the front foot slides forward. The degree of power used may vary. Light, fast punches are used to feint or to test an opponent's defense. More powerful Jabs are used to keep an opponent off-balance, prevent an attacker from moving in, set up combinations, or execute crippling blows. Remember, speed is inversely proportional to power. As you generate more power, speed diminishes and recovery time increases. While a Jab Punch can be a finishing blow, it is usually used to set up more powerful rear-hand strikes. Traditional Jabs develop power by retracting the opposite hand to the hip, which also sets up the next strike, usually a straight punch. Balance is equal between both feet. Modern Jabs are executed from a high guard, with the rear hand remaining in guard position. Reach increases by shifting balance to the front foot, as the rear foot pushes forward, rising onto the ball. A comparison between traditional and modern Jab Punches is shown on the preceding page.

2. Straight Punch

Straight Punches are thrusting strikes in which all power is focused on hitting through a target directly ahead. The punching hand follows a straight line and is rotated between 45° to 180° during delivery. This twisting motion focuses power and may produce a cutting effect on face targets. The strike is executed with either hand, from any stance, while stationary or moving in any direction.

Fore Fist

Jab Punch to cheekbone at SI-18

Straight Punch to SP-21, slipping attacker's punch

Punching power depends on arm speed, hip and shoulder rotation, and rear leg thrust. When executing rear hand punches (most powerful), the shoulder leads and the punch follows. Hip and shoulder rotation is often exaggerated, with the rear leg pivoting on the ball of the foot for greater power and reach.

The following names are often used to designate specific types of Straight Punches: A rear hand punch is often called a *reverse punch* or *cross punch*. A Straight Punch executed at the end of a forward step, with the punching hand on the same side as forward foot, is often called a *lunge punch*. Today, lunge punches are mostly used in training to develop timing and use of the hips. In modern combat, lunge punches are usually too slow to be practical unless well set up.

3. Vertical Punch

A Vertical Punch is a snapping strike similar to a Straight Punch, except the hand finishes in a vertical position. When punching from from a traditional guard (palm up), the fist rotates about 90° during delivery; from a modern guard, not at all. Some martial artists feel that it is possible to hit harder and faster with the Vertical Punch due to the reduced hand rotation. For this reason, it is often used to deliver fast combinations at close range.

4. Overhead Punch

An Overhead Punch (or *overhead cross*) is a powerful thrusting Fore Fist strike, usually executed with the rear hand (lead strikes are possible, but rarely used). The fist travels forward and a little downward in a slightly circular motion, with the hand rotating up to 180°. Execute by raising the elbow with the palm facing down, immediately thrusting the shoulder and upper arm forward. On impact, the arm may be partially bent or extended, based on target range. Power is generated by hip and shoulder rotation, with rear leg thrust. Transfer your weight to the front leg, with the rear heel raised on impact. Think of the delivery as a forward and downward chopping motion. This punch is often used to cross over an opponent's jab, or hook over top of their guard.

Vertical Punch while pulling attacker into strike

Overhead Punch to joint of jaw at ST-7

5. Hook Punch

In a Hook Punch, the Fore Fist follows a horizontal circular path, with the elbow bent throughout the strike. The degree to which the elbow is bent determines the range of the strike. The punching hand rotates anywhere between 45° and 180°, finishing level with the elbow. Do not take too wide a swing, as this slows execution, telegraphs the punch, and opens you to counterattacks. Do not pull the hand back to prepare; punch directly from your guard. Hook Punches can be executed with either hand, and are often delivered by stepping sideways as this assists the swing. Power is generated by shoulder and hip rotation, leg thrust, and by transferring weight to the opposite leg. On lead hooks, the front foot pivots and the rear foot is weighted. On rear hooks, the front foot is weighted and the rear foot pivots. Targets include the groin, ribs, and head. A long-range Hook Punch (elbow extended) is also called a *roundhouse punch* in some martial arts.

6. Uppercut Punch

The Uppercut Punch is a close range strike. The Fore Fist follows an upward or straight path, with the fist inverted. It is executed with either hand, with the fist rotating about 90°. The elbow usually remains bent, although it can be extended for reach. Targets include the groin, torso, and underside of the chin.

Fore Fist

Hook Punch to chin at ST-4

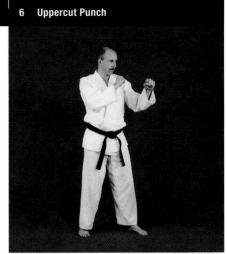

Uppercut Punch to ribs and kidney at GB-25

7. Back Punch

In a Back Punch, the fist takes a circular path from the hip over the opposite shoulder, to hit an opponent very close behind you. The arm is bent throughout, with the hand rotating 180°. Power and distance comes from shoulder rotation, retracting the opposite hand to the hip, and sometimes a step back. The punch is useful against a choke, hold, or during ground fighting, when an attacker's face is close to your shoulder. When standing, the retracting arm becomes a simultaneous elbow strike to the belly or solar plexus.

8. Rising Punch

In a Rising Punch, the extended arm is raised upward in a circular path, often with a slight forward thrust. Power is generated by arm speed combined with natural shoulder and hip turn. Rising Punches are usually disguised strikes executed from relaxed or walking stances to a stationary or charging opponent. Against a charge, time the strike so that the attacker runs into the blow. When punching, the Fore Fist may face either up or down. Palm-down targets include the groin, chin, and underside of the attacking arm. Palm-up targets include the face, ribs, and chest.

Back Punch to chin, elbow strike to stomach or ribs

Rising Punch to underside of chin and throat

51

9–12 Back Fist Strikes

The Back Fist hand formation is the same as a Fore Fist, except you will bend the wrist back slightly and strike with the tops of the first two knuckles. Back Fist strikes can be executed with either hand (lead is most common), to targets anywhere on the body. The protruding knuckles make it well suited for hitting sensitive nerves or pressure points.

9. Outside Back Fist

The Back Fist follows an outward circular path, using either a snapping or thrusting delivery. In the snapping version, the Back Fist *snaps* forward and is quickly retracted on impact, as the fist traces a circular path, with the elbow acting as a fulcrum. Begin with the elbow fully bent and the wrist cocked, or strike directly from guard without cocking the elbow. Power comes from the coordinated snap of the elbow and wrist. The opposite arm may be retracted to add power. Because of its speed, this strike is often used like a jab to set up combinations, or as a striking-block to thrusting punches.

In the thrusting variation, elbow snap is reduced, body rotation is increased, and the fist hits *through* the target. A longer delivery and follow-through will generate greater power, particularly if preceded by a turn step or body spin. Soft targets such as the side of the body or neck are preferred, since power strikes to the skull may break your knuckles unless the bone has been conditioned. When power-hitting, the *Hammer Fist* is preferred, since it withstands greater impact without damaging your hand.

Back Fist

Snap Back Fist to temple at M-HN-9

Descending blow to nose bridge (M-HN-3 or M-HN-4)

10. Descending Back Fist

The fist follows a downward circular path, usually to the face, nose (M-HN-3 and M-HN-4), upper lip (GV-26) or chin (CO-24). Use either a snapping delivery (retracting the hand), or a thrusting delivery (hitting through the target).

11. Rising Back Fist

The Back Fist follows an upward circular path, using either a snapping or thrusting delivery. Targets include the groin, underside of attacking arm or chin, or the face or chest of a bent-over opponent. It is also useful for hitting an attacker behind you.

12. Raking Back Fist

This is a glancing or raking strike used to hit one or more targets in a single delivery. The Back Fist rotates 180°, as you snap the fist downward and inward toward your body. It is usually used to hit nerves or pressure points on the face, chest, inner forearm, biceps, or leg. The photo at the lower-right shows a raking strike to pressure points on the inner arm, hitting PC-2, LU-5, M-UE-31, and M-UE-32.

Rising Back Fist to testicles

Raking strike to nerves along inner arm

13–16 Hammer Fist Strikes

There are three Hammer Fist formations: Hammer Fist, Loose Hammer Fist, and Ki Hammer Fist. In all three, the hitting surface is the bottom fleshy part of the fist. The first version, *Hammer Fist,* is a tightly clenched fist, identical to the Fore Fist. It is used in many martial arts. The others, *Loose Hammer Fist* and *Ki Hammer Fist,* are used in Hapkido and some energy-oriented arts. In both versions, the fist is partially clenched, with the index and thumb fingers loose. Relaxing the upper part of the fist results in greater speed and fluidity as the arm musculature is more relaxed. However, since the fist is partially loose, it is more easily damaged by inaccurate striking or unintentional clashing. When executing fast transitions between Fore Fist, Back Fist, and Hammer Fist

Hammer Fist

Loose Hammer Fist

Ki Hammer Fist

Outside Hammer Fist to base of skull at BL-10 or GB-20

Descending Hammer Fist to base of skull and neck

strikes, use the first version. The Loose Hammer and Ki Hammer are less practical, since the hand must be reformed between strikes, which slows execution and adds unnecessary complexity. The Hammer Fist is one of the most powerful hand strikes, based on its ability to sustain impact without damage. This is due to the amount of tissue and muscle present at the base of the hand. In contrast, the Back Fist is more easily damaged, but is superior in focusing force over a much smaller area, which is more useful when hitting pressure points.

Hammer Fists are executed using inward, outward, rising, descending, or angular deliveries. The Hammer Fist does not require extensive surface conditioning or the precise wrist alignment required to use a Fore Fist safely. This makes it useful for novices and a preferred technique for critical situations in which a broken knuckle, sustained during a Back Fist or Fore Fist strike, becomes a severe liability.

13. Outside Hammer Fist
The delivery is identical to the *Outside Back Fist* (see preceding pages).

14. Descending Hammer Fist
The fist follows a downward circular path. Begin with the fist cocked behind the ear, or raised overhead. Strike forward and down, fully rotating the shoulders as you sink the hips. The fist twists about 135°. Targets include the face, bridge of nose, forehead (GV-24), collarbone, spine, or skull.

15. Inside Hammer Fist
The fist follows an inward circular path (horizontal or angular). Begin with the elbow bent; snap the fist forward extending the elbow and rotating the fist about 180°. Power is generated by arm twist, body turn, and leg thrust. A full delivery begins with the fist cocked behind the ear. Shorter, deliveries are also possible, striking directly from a guard. Targets include the temple, side of nose, jaw, neck, ribs, spine, base of skull, and kneecap (dislocates laterally).

16. Twin Hammer Fist
Hammer Fist Strikes can also be executed simultaneously to one or more opponents. Examples are shown at the far right.

Inside Hammer Fist to kidney and ribs

Twin Inside Hammer Fist to floating ribs

Twin Outside Hammer Fist to noses

HAND STRIKES
    17   Outside Thumb Fist
    18   Inside Thumb Fist

17–20 Thumb Fist Strikes

The Thumb Fist hand formation is the same as the Fore Fist, except the protruding thumb is placed on top, pressing down against the index finger for support. The hitting surfaces are the point of, or area between, the thumb knuckles. Since thumb surfaces cannot withstand hard impact without damage, they are primarily used for medium to light blows, to soft or highly sensitive areas. Targets include the temple, lips, face, neck, ribs, or any other protected areas where nerves or pressure points are present. The arm muscles are tensed on impact, with the wrist firmly locked and the fist tightly clenched. Keep the thumbnail trimmed very short as it tends to cut into the supporting index finger on impact. The Thumb Fist formation can also be used in place of the Fore Fist, Back Fist, or Hammer Fist. In these instances make contact with the first two fist knuckles, or bottom of fist. Some Okinawan and Chinese styles favor the Thumb Fist over the Fore Fist, since placement of the thumb on top helps prevent the fist from buckling at the wrist on impact. This is useful for persons with weaker wrists. In Hapkido, it is mostly used for hitting with the thumb knuckle.

17. Outside Thumb Fist

The forearm twists and snaps, sideways and forward, from inside to outside. The Thumb Fist rotates 90°–180° during delivery, as the thumb snaps into the target. When striking at very close range, the delivery resembles the motion of an outside block. Power comes from the snap and twist of the lower arm assisted by a short body turn.

Thumb Fist

Outside Thumb Fist to side of ribs at SP-21

Inside Thumb Fist to back of jaw at TW-17

18. Inside Thumb Fist

The Thumb Fist follows an inward circular path (horizontal or angular).The strike can be executed with the arm extended, partially bent, or by beginning with the arm extended and snapping the elbow closed (about 90°) on impact. When grappling or fighting at close range, this last method can also be used to reach around and strike pressure points on the spine, back, or base of the skull (e.g., BL-10). Power is generated by arm speed, body rotation, and the accelerated speed of the fist caused by snapping the elbow closed.

19. Rising Thumb Fist

Similar to an *Inside Thumb Fist,* except the fist follows an upward circular path. Targets include the groin (while standing or kneeling), the underside of an attacker's extended arm, or the face or throat of a bent-over opponent.

20. Twin Thumb Fist

Thumb Fist Strikes can also be executed simultaneously to one or more opponents. Examples are shown at the far right. The Twin Outside Thumb Fist Strike requires very little space for delivery, and is quite practical at close range when crowded.

Rising Thumb Fist striking upward to groin at CO-1

Twin Inside Thumb Fist to temples at TW-23 (break choke)

Twin Outside Thumb Fist to GB-25 at kidneys

21–24 Finger Knuckle Strikes

There are four hand formations which use the second set of finger knuckles for hitting: Middle Finger Fist, Index Finger Fist, Knuckle Fist, and Knuckle Hand. They can be executed using any of the eight deliveries outlined previously under *Fore Fist Strikes.* Since the hitting surfaces cannot withstand forceful impact without damage, these strikes are primarily used for medium to light blows to soft or highly sensitive areas, where the profile of the protruding knuckles permits greater penetration than the Fore Fist allows. Targets include the temple, eyes, nerve at the upper lip, face, neck, ribs, groin, knee, or any other protected areas where nerves or pressure points are present.

When striking, the arm muscles are tensed on impact, with the wrist firmly locked and fist tightly clenched. The photographs at right and on the next page show a range of possible applications. Various methods of delivery were covered earlier under *Fore Fist Strikes.* Straight or hooking motions are most typical.

21. Middle Finger Fist

This formation is basically a Fore Fist with the second knuckle of the middle finger extended. Bend the wrist slightly backward so that the knuckle is protruding forward. Make sure the wrist is firmly locked since the inner tendons are easily damaged (by stretching) if the wrist is allowed to bend further backwards during the strike. Also, the hand must also be tightly clenched or you will damage the finger joints from movement at impact. Strike with the point of the knuckle.

Middle Finger Fist striking upward to SI-18 on cheek

Middle Finger Fist (to nerve at inner knee at SP-10)

Twin Middle Finger Fist (to nerves along ribs, SP-21)

Index Finger Fist (to nerve at temple, TW-23)

Index Finger Fist (to nerves on back of hand, TW-3)

Twin Index Finger Fist (to cheek at SI-18 or ST-3)

Middle Finger Fist

Index Finger Fist

22. Index Finger Fist

This fist is formed with the second knuckle of the index finger extended. The protruding finger is braced by pressing down with the thumb on top. This prevents damage to the index finger base-joint from finger movement during impact. This strike can be used in place of the Middle Finger Fist, particularly if the fist cannot be tightly clenched.

23. Knuckle Fist

The Knuckle Fist is formed the same as the Thumb Fist, except you strike with the second set of four knuckles, and bend the wrist slightly backward so that the knuckles are protruding forward. Make sure the wrist is firmly locked, since the inner tendons are easily damaged (by stretching) if the wrist is allowed to bend further back during the blow. This strike is also called a *knuckle punch.*

24. Knuckle Hand

This is similar to a Knuckle Fist, except the hand is partially open and aligned with the forearm. Form by pressing the fingertips against the palm, with the hand slightly bent. Contact area is the same as with the Knuckle Fist and is used for similar purposes. Because your are striking with the tips of all four knuckles, it is possible to hit several pressure points simultaneously. For example, ST-9 and ST-10 at the throat, or LV-12 and SP-12 in the groin (see photos). When compared to *clenched fist* strikes, the Knuckle Hand has a narrow profile, allowing it to slip in where a fist might not fit (e.g., striking the throat at CO-23 when the chin is held low).

Knuckle Fist (Uppercut Punch to top of throat)

Knuckle Fist (punch and grind to nerve at lip at GV-26)

Twin Knuckle Fist (to both sides of neck at LI-18)

Knuckle Hand (to throat at ST-9 and ST-10)

Knuckle Hand (to groin area)

Twin Knuckle Hand (to ST-9 at neck and LV-13 at ribs)

Knuckle Fist

Knuckle Hand

25–27 Knife Hand Strikes

A Knife Hand is formed by extending the fingers with a slight bend at the second set of knuckles. Press the fingers tightly together, press the thumb against the palm, and tense the hand and wrist. The hitting surface is the fleshy edge of the tensed hand, or the base knuckle of the fifth finger when hitting pressure points. Knife Hand strikes are executed using the same delivery motions as the Hammer Fist, using either the lead or rear hand (inside, outside, snapping, descending, rising). Targets include the temple, neck, back of the skull, and side of the torso. The arm muscles are tensed on impact with the wrist firmly locked. Power is generated by arm speed combined with hip and shoulder rotation. Historically, Hapkido Knife Hand strikes were executed with an extended arm, long circular delivery, and fully rotated hips and shoulders, with the entire body committed to the strike. The extended arm is often compared to a sword.

25. Outside Knife Hand

The strike follows an outward circular path, using either a snapping or thrusting delivery, similar to the *Outside Back Fist* shown previously. The hips and shoulders may either rotate *with* the strike; or in the *opposite* direction of the strike, particularly when stepping forward or back from a relaxed stance to a side stance. In snapping deliveries, the hand *snaps* forward and is quickly retracted on impact, as the fist traces a circular path. In thrusting deliveries, elbow snap is reduced, body rotation is increased, and the hand hits *through* the target for greater power.

Knife Hand

Outside Knife Hand to temple

Inside Knife Hand to sternocleidomastoid muscle

26. Inside Knife Hand
Delivery is similar to the Inside Hammer Fist. Rotate the Knife Hand at least 180° during the strike. Snap the edge of the hand into the target, as you turn the hips and shoulders in unison.

27. Descending Knife Hand
The hand follows a downward circular path, identical to the *Descending Hammer Fist*. The arm may be partially bent or fully extended. In Hapkido, the upper body leans into the strike to provide additional power, as shown in the third photo. In many other martial arts, the upper body will remain upright, over the hips, as shown in the fourth photo.

28. Cutting Hand

This is a slashing strike using the fingernails of the Knife Hand to cut or abrade soft tissue such as the eyes, ears, nose, lips, face, or throat. Draw the fingernails quickly across the target surface. There should be no hard impact. Add only enough depth to the strike to cut, scratch or abrade the skin. If you strike too deep, you may stress the finger joints sideways, damaging ligaments or dislocating joints. Hand speed and accuracy are the most important factors, although long fingernails are also an asset. Delivery is outward with the elbow acting as a fulcrum, and the wrist and hand tensed at impact. The Cutting Hand is mostly used as a distraction or an initial surprise strike, often from relaxed stances.

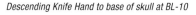

Cutting Hand

Descending Knife Hand to base of skull at BL-10

Cutting Hand slashing both eyes with fingernails

29–32 Spear Hand

Spear Hands are thrusting strikes using the fingertips to attack pressure points, or soft areas such as the eyes, throat, armpit, and groin. Speed and accuracy are more important than power, as fingers withstand little impact. Keep the fingers flexed to prevent joint damage from unyielding targets. Fast jabs to the eyes are often used to set up other techniques. The four Spear Hand formations are shown below. Their use is covered in the *Fundamentals* chapter, under *Attack Points*.

33–34 Back Hand

There are three Back Hand formations: Relaxed Back Hand, Tense Back Hand, and Ki Back Hand. In all three, the hitting surface is the back of the hand. In the first version, *Relaxed Back Hand,* the fingers and wrist remain relaxed throughout the strike. This version allows for greater speed and fluidity than the other two, as the arm musculature is more relaxed. In the second two, *Tense Back Hand* and *Ki Back Hand,* the hand and wrist are rigidly tensed on impact, and align with the forearm. Tensing musculature permits greater force without damaging the hand or wrist.

Back Hand strikes use either a thrusting or a circular snapping delivery. This blow is useful as a surprise or disguised first strike from a relaxed stance. It might also be used to execute a forceful strike to the ribs in place of the Back Fist. For example, this could become necessary if your finger joints are damaged during a fight and you can no longer close your hand to form a fist. Two basic deliveries are described next. Many others are also possible.

29. Spear Hand (to throat, ST-9 and ST-10)

29. Spear Hand (to groin at SP-12 and LV-12)

Fast lead jab to the eyes (use any Spear Hand)

30. Spear Hand – 2 Fingers (to eye and/or GB-1)

31. Spear Hand – 2 Fingers Spread (to both eyes)

32. Spear Hand –1 Finger (to base of throat at CO-22)

Spear Hand

Spear Hand – 2 Fingers

Spear Hand – 2 Fingers Spread

Spear Hand – 1 Finger

33. Straight Back Hand

This strike uses a very fast thrusting or snapping delivery to soft targets on the groin, midsection, or face—usually in fast combinations with other strikes or blocks. The hand follows a straight path and snaps forward into the target by bending at the wrist on impact. Speed is the most important factor. Use the Relaxed Back Hand formation.

34. Circular Back Hand

Delivery is identical to the *Back Fist Strike* described earlier in this chapter. In this outward circular strike the elbow acts as a fulcrum. Use any of the three Back Hand formations (shown below), although the Tense Back Hand and Ki Back Hand are more often preferred for power and safety.

Relaxed Back Hand

Tense Back Hand

Ki Back Hand

Straight Back Hand to side of head (hand relaxed)

Circular Back Hand to ribs and solar plexus (hand tensed)

35. Ridge Hand

The Ridge Hand is similar to a Knife Hand, except you tuck the thumb further in against the palm and hit with the tensed inner edge of the hand, or the base knuckles of the index finger and thumb if hitting pressure points. The hand rotates about 90° during delivery and usually follows an inward or forward circular path, with the arm extended at impact (elbow slightly flexed to prevent hyperextension). Targets include the bridge and base of the nose, the lips, neck, throat, temple, and ribs. You can also strike using a hooking motion: the arm begins extended and rapidly snaps inward to about 90°. This version is usually used at close range.

36. Ox Jaw Hand

The Ox Jaw is basically a forward thrusting Knife Hand strike. Thrust the fingertips toward the target. Just before impact, bend the hand sideways at the wrist, thrusting the outer edge of hand into the target. The outside edge of the hand and wrist should form a curve, imitating an ox's jaw. The Ox Jaw is usually used to strike the sides of nose, jaw or neck; solar plexus; collarbone; or to block a punch.

Ridge Hand

Ox Jaw Hand

Ridge Hand to throat at ST-9 and ST-10

Ox Jaw Hand to collarbone and brachial plexus

37. Chicken Hand

The Chicken Hand is usually delivered by snapping or swinging the hand upward into the armpit or underside of an attacker's extended arm. Horizontal strikes to head or neck pressure-points are also practical. Form a Knife Hand with the fingers and thumb flexed inward, and the wrist bent sideways, opposite of an Ox Jaw Hand. This formation resembles a chicken's head, hence its name. Execute with the arm bent or extended, striking with the base and first joint of the thumb, rigidly tensing the wrist on impact to prevent joint damage.

38. Tiger Mouth Hand

This is usually a thrusting strike to the throat, which shifts to a hold by squeezing the windpipe with the thumb and fingers (like a tiger gripping its prey). It can also be used to strike up to the groin (squeezing testicles), or to break the elbow of a held arm. Form a Knife Hand with the thumb widely separated. Contact area is between the tip of the thumb and the first knuckle of the index finger. The strike is applied from any direction, finishing with the palm facing up, down, or sideways. A straight thrust with the palm down is most common.

Chicken Hand

Tiger Mouth Hand

Chicken Hand to TW-11 near back of elbow

Tiger Mouth Strike to throat, then squeezing

39–43 Palm Heel Hand

The Palm Heel Hand is a powerful thrusting or snapping strike using the base of the palm to attack targets anywhere on the body, from any direction (rising, descending, circular, straight). The strike may be applied from any posture with lead or rear hands, and is often used instead of a fist when punching—jab, straight, hook, uppercut, overhead, and twin deliveries are possible. Palm Heels are commonly used to strike the chest, solar plexus, ribs, spine, jaw, nose, or head, or to break joints. It is one of the more powerful hand strikes, based on its ability to sustain impact without damage. It is easily learned and is particularly recommended for women or small individuals facing larger opponents.

39. Straight Palm Heel

Keep the wrist and arm relaxed as your hand thrusts toward the target. Just before impact, snap the wrist forward to add force to the strike (sometimes with a twisting motion of the hand). Use either a snapping or thrusting delivery, with the arm bent or extended based on target distance. Power is generated by coordinating hip and shoulder rotation, arm speed, and pronounced wrist snap.

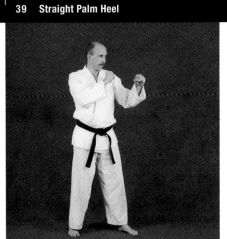

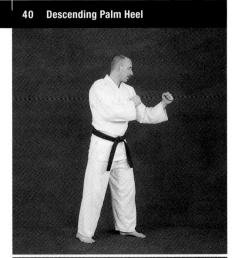

Palm Heel Hand

Straight Palm Heel to jaw

Descending Palm Heel to bridge of nose at M-HN-4

40. Descending Palm Heel

This strike is mostly used to break the nose by striking the bridge downward from the front. The relaxed hand is brought straight down, snapping the wrist downward just before impact. This strike often follows a bent wrist strike (to the chin) or jab (if the attacker ducks), since these blows ideally position the hand for a Palm Heel. It is easy to break the nose with this strike, so practice with caution.

41. Uppercut Palm Heel

Similar to an Uppercut Punch, the hand traces an upward circular path with the elbow bent about 90° throughout. Power comes from arm speed, shoulder and hip rotation, and leg thrust. At close range, disguise the delivery by bringing the hand upward, close to the opponent's body. Targets include the abdomen, floating ribs, underside of the chin, or the elbow of a held arm. When the opponent is bent over, the face and chest are also targets.

42. Hook Palm Heel

Similar to a Hook Punch, the hand follows an inward circular path (horizontal or angular), with the fingers pointing inward. The target is usually the side of the nose or jaw, or the ribs. Use either the lead or rear hand, keeping your elbow approximately at the level of your hand.

The *Inside Palm Heel Strike*, which also uses an inward circular motion, is shown on the next page.

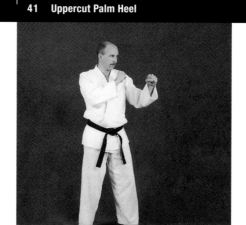

Uppercut Palm Heel to underside of jaw (whiplash)

Hook Palm Heel to side of nose

43. Inside Palm Heel

This is an inward circular strike similar to the previous *Hook Palm Heel,* except the fingers face outward. Extend the arm based on range. It is often used to hit the temple, side of the jaw, side of the nose, back of jaw at its joint, rear base of the skull, floating ribs, kidneys, and spine.

44. Open Hand

Open Hand strikes (also called palm strikes) use the entire palm to strike a broad area. The hand may be formed in one of two ways: 1) by extending the fingers and stretching the palm to tighten the striking surface, or 2) by extending the fingers and cupping the palm.

Targets include the tip of nose, side of jaw, ear, and groin. When striking the groin (often to assist certain throws), use an upward circular motion between the legs. When striking the ears (often against a choke), puncture the ear drums by slapping both tightened-palms inward over both ear holes. Strikes to the nose and mouth easily shift to smothering holds. Slaps to the face can be used as a distraction to set up other attacks.

Ki is believed to collect in the center of the palm, which is one of the points where some people believe it enters and exits the body. In martial arts, Open Hand strikes can be used to project destructive Ki into the target on impact, thereby increasing a strike's efficiency. In Eastern medicine, healers apply the same principle, using their hands to manipulate a patient's Ki. Transferring Ki is said to require extensive training and emotional control, as well as genetic gifts.

45. Bear Hand

This strike uses the entire palm to hit a broad area. Use either a straight thrust or circular sweeping motion. This blow combines both hitting and tearing in a single motion, similar to how a bear uses its claws. Form the hand by bending and pressing the fingertips inward against the palm, stretching the palm to tighten the surface. Target is usually the face, eyes, and ears. After striking, the fingers can be used to grab or tear skin and clothing.

Bear Fist

A variation of the Bear Hand hand formation, called a *Bear Fist*, is formed by clenching the hand in a fist, in the same manner as the Thumb Fist. You will strike with the flat inner-surface of your fist. Make sure your thumb is on top, as shown at the bottom of the next page (see Bear Fist). If you form a fist with the thumb on the inner side (Fore Fist), you may damage it on impact. Use an inward circular delivery and snap your wrist forward as you swing your forearm.

46. Claw Hand

This is classified as a raking strike and is used to scratch, cut, gouge, or tear soft or protruding tissue and clothing. Apply by dragging or gouging the tips or fingernails of all five fingers across targets, such as the eyes, ears, lips, nostrils, face, and neck. Palm Heel, Open Hand, and Bear Hand strikes often shift to Claw Hands to secure a face hold or assist a throw or takedown (see photos on next page).

Palm Heel Hand

Inside Palm Heel to side of nose

Open Hand (straight thrust to nose)

Bear Hand (inward to ear and side of head)

Claw Hand (to eyes and pressure points on face)

Open Hand (rising strike to groin)

Bear Hand (downward to front of face and eyes)

Claw Hand (gouging pressure points on neck and face)

Twin Open Hand (puncturing both ear drums)

Bear Hand (straight thrust to jaw, ear, and eye)

Claw Hand (grabbing groin, clawing eye and face)

Open Hand

Bear Hand

Bear Fist

Claw Hand

47. Five Fingertip Hand

This is a straight or circular strike used to hit nerve clusters or multiple targets over a broad area. Form by partially bending all five fingertips inward, similar to a Claw Hand, but with the fingers more extended. Make contact with all five fingertips simultaneously. Targets include the eyes, face, Adam's apple, ribs, armpit, and groin. Take the same precautions to protect finger joints as you would with a Spear Hand.

48. Thumb Hand

A Thumb Hand is a circular strike used for pinpoint attacks to highly sensitive areas. Form a relaxed fist with the thumb rigidly extended (locked or bent), using the tip to strike the eyes, throat, nerves, or pressure points. The strike is executed using any delivery outlined under *Thumb Fist* strikes, although inside circular motions (palm down) are most common. Because the fist is partially formed, Thumb Hands can quickly change to and from Fore Fist strikes. When compared to other finger strikes, such as Spear Hands or the Five Fingertip Hand, the Thumb Hand is one of the strongest in its ability to withstand impact without damage. Nonetheless, take precautions to protect the finger joints as you would with other spearing strikes.

Five Fingertip Hand

Thumb Hand

Five Fingertip Hand to eyes and pressure points on face

Thumb Hand to throat at ST-9 or CO-22

49. Pincer Hand

This is a thrusting and clamping strike using the tips of the bent thumb and index fingers, in the manner of a crab's claw. The other three fingers are clenched and can be used for hitting if desired. Targets include the Adam's apple, cavity at base of throat, brachial plexus, cheek pressure points, both sides of the mouth (press cheeks into teeth), nerves at the top of the larynx (knuckles hit throat), both eyes (knuckles hit mouth), and Achilles tendon (to release a leg hold). It can also be used to pinch or pull the nose, lips, ears, body hair, or other sensitive skin (e.g., pinching the side of waist to release a hold). Pinching a small amount of skin is usually more painful.

50. Eagle Hand

This is a snapping strike using the clustered tips of all five fingers to attack sensitive areas, or to reach targets at difficult angles. Execute by snapping the hand forward at the wrist, using deliveries from any direction. Arm motion is primarily used to position the hand, not for power. Targets include the temple, eyes, jaw joint, throat, solar plexus, armpit, nerves along ribs, and groin. This strike resembles the manner in which a bird uses its beak. It is also called *peacock hand* and *eagle's beak*.

Pincer Hand

Eagle Hand

Pincer Hand to windpipe (striking and squeezing)

Eagle Hand to GB-25 near end of 12th floating rib

1–4 Bent Wrist Strikes

These are thrusting, snapping, or circular strikes using the back of the bent wrist to hit targets anywhere on the body, from any direction (straight, inward, outward, rising). Begin with the wrist straight, snapping it into the target by bending the wrist. The arm and hand remain relaxed throughout the strike, to promote speed and fluidity. These techniques are often used as disguised strikes or blocks, from relaxed stances or walking postures. Since the hands are unformed, they are easy for novices to learn and are excellent substitutes for closed-hand strikes if your hand is damaged.

1. Straight Bent Wrist Strike

This strike uses a straight thrusting or snapping delivery to targets on the midsection or head—usually in very fast combinations with other strikes or blocks. The delivery is the same as the *Straight Back Hand* strike outlined previously.

2. Outside Bent Wrist Strike

The wrist follows a circular path from inside outward, to strike targets 45° forward, or to the side. Targets include the ribs, solar plexus, temple, ears, or face.

3. Inside Bent Wrist Strike

The wrist follows an inward circular path, with the arm bent or extended based on target distance. Targets include the ribs, throat, jaw, nose, or side of the head.

4. Rising Bent Wrist Strike

The hand follows a rising vertical path to targets such as the groin, underside of chin, or underside of an attacker's punching arm. The arm is extended throughout the delivery as it swings upward into the target, using the shoulder as a fulcrum. The technique is often used as a disguised strike from a relaxed or walking stance. Power is generated by arm speed, wrist snap, and shoulder rotation.

5–6 Inner and Outer Wrist Strikes

These surfaces are primarily used for applying chokes. However, they can also be used to strike pressure points or nerves, or to enter a choke-hold forcefully by hitting into the neck as you wrap it.

7. Outer Forearm Strike

This powerful strike uses the ulna bone on the outer forearm for strikes or hard blocks, usually at closer distances. Forearm muscles are tensed on impact by using a fist or any tensed open-hand formation. In Hapkido, a *stepped fist* is preferred (see photo), which tenses different forearm muscles. Because the stepped fist is more difficult to form, and requires a transition to or from other hand formations, it requires practice. However, it does permit greater speed and fluidity, since the arm is more relaxed.

The outer forearm is commonly used to strike the head, jaw, throat, ribs, elbow (break joint), knees, and leg tendons. When compared to hand strikes, the bone can withstand greater impact without damage, which makes it excellent for smaller individuals facing overpowering opponents. However, you must use your hitting surfaces accurately, since contact on the inside or outside of the forearm can easily damage sensitive nerves and tendons. This strike can be applied using any delivery outlined under *Hammer Fist Strikes* (inside, outside, rising, descending, thrusting snapping, circular).

8. Inner Forearm Strike

This strike uses the radius bone on the inner forearm for circular strikes or hard blocks (inward, outward or rising). This strike is often used for elbow breaks or clothesline strikes to the front of the face or throat. In a clothesline strike, you allow your opponent's forward momentum to carry him or her into your extended arm. Keep the elbow flexed to prevent hyper-extension, and rotate your shoulders for additional force. A rising strike to the groin is often used to assist certain throws in which upward lift is important.

9. Hook Forearm Strike

The inner forearm is usually used at close range to reach around and strike targets on the unexposed side. The elbow acts as a fulcrum, as your extended forearm snaps closed. Pressure points on the back of the head and face are the usual targets. It can also be used to break the elbow of a held arm or blocked punch.

Bent Wrist

Inner Wrist

Outer Wrist

Outer Forearm

Inner Forearm

1. Straight Bent Wrist Strike (to solar plexus)

2. Outside Bent Wrist Strike (to temple)

3. Inside Bent Wrist Strike (to jaw)

4. Rising Bent Wrist Strike (to groin area)

5. Inner Wrist Strike (changes into a choke)

6. Outer Wrist Strike (to throat and underside of chin)

7. Outer Forearm Strike (outside circular delivery)

7. Outer Forearm Strike (thrusting delivery to nose)

7. Outer Forearm Strike (to back of knee, throw)

8. Inner Forearm Strike (clothesline to throat)

9. Hook Forearm Strike (to back of head)

9. Hook Forearm Strike (elbow break)

Elbow strikes are one of the most powerful methods for delivering blows. They can be executed in any direction, to any target, and are an essential technique for anyone facing overpowering opponents. Normally used at close range, they are very effective at creating space when you are being held or crowded. Elbow strikes are fairly easy to learn and apply, and are valuable in any self-defense system. Hit with the bony area around the point of the elbow. Take care to protect the ulna nerve (funny bone), as it is easily damaged if struck. Power is created by body rotation, arm speed, and use of upper body muscles. Sometimes the hand twists up to 180° to aid timing and power.

1. Rising Elbow Strike

The elbow follows an upward circular path, striking with the Lower Elbow. Use the shoulders, hips, and upward leg thrust to assist the strike. Targets include the solar plexus, spine, or underside of the chin.

2. Descending Elbow Strike

The elbow follows a downward circular path on a vertical axis, striking with the Upper Elbow. Use forward body momentum and/or the sinking of your shoulders and hips to generate power. Targets include the face, collarbone, brachial plexus, sternum, shoulder, the head or spine of a bent-over opponent, or the joints of a held arm or leg.

3. Inside Elbow Strike

The elbow follows a horizontal or angular circular path from outside-inward, striking with the Lower Elbow to targets directly forward or 45° to the side. This is likely the most powerful arm strike, since the hitting surface can withstand substantial impact without damage, and the entire body powers the strike. Body rotation creates power. Targets include the head, chest, ribs, spleen, kidney, spine, and knees.

4. Outside Elbow Strike

The elbow follows an outward, horizontal or angular path, striking with the Upper Elbow to targets directly forward or 90° to the side. Use body rotation and arm speed to create power. Take care to protect the ulna nerve by striking near the point of the elbow, preferably to soft areas. Target the chest, solar plexus, ribs, kidney, and head.

Rising Elbow Strike to underside of jaw

Descending Elbow Strike to spine

Hand Formations

Elbow strikes may be applied using a range of different hand formations, including closed hands (relaxed), open hands (relaxed or tensed), or a Live-Hand. Select the option that provides the quickest transition to the next technique. A clenched fist is usually not used, since the tensed forearm tends to slow delivery and reduce follow-through.

Upper Elbow (closed-hand option)

Upper Elbow (open-hand option)

Upper Elbow (Live-Hand option)

Lower Elbow (closed-hand option)

Inside Elbow Strike to ribs

Outside Elbow to throat (note arm lock and stomp)

5. Assisted Inside Elbow Strike

This two-handed technique uses your free hand to block, protect, or add power to an inside circular strike. To execute, clasp the hands together, with palm against palm. Create power by stepping forward and rotating your entire body into the strike. The striking elbow follows a horizontal path with the supporting forearm finishing vertical, as it blocks or protects against incoming punches. This method is also used to break a straight-arm choke while striking the jaw. Since the wrists are close together, this strike is useful even when your hands are tightly tied together.

6. Assisted Side Elbow Strike

This two-handed technique uses your free hand to add power to a thrusting strike directed sideways. To strike toward the right side, thrust the point of your right elbow straight sideways, with your left palm pushing against your right fist. Use body momentum, arm speed, and a side step to generate power. Common targets include the face, eye, throat, solar plexus, spine, and sternum. This strike is also useful if your hands are tied or cuffed.

Grip for technique 5

Grip for technique 6

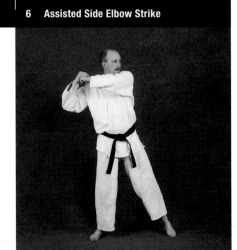

Inside strike to jaw, support arm breaking choke hold

Assisted Side Elbow Strike to throat

7. Back Elbow Strike
Use a backward thrusting motion to hit an opponent behind you. Body rotation and arm speed generate power as you step backward. Concentrate on pulling the hand to the waist, rather than driving the elbow. When executing two or more strikes, snap the hips in the *opposite* direction of the strike, for speed and power. The strike's path is usually straight to the midsection or groin; however, a rising strike to the underside of the chin is also possible.

8. Inner Elbow Strike
Execute a short snapping strike by extending your hand outward as the inner elbow thrusts forward. Your arm begins bent and finishes extended. This strike is only useful at close range if properly set up. There are three specialized applications:

A. Strike to Back-of-Head: Execute a snapping strike to the back of the head at the skull-neck junction. Unclenched teeth will usually slam shut, often cutting the tongue or mouth.

B. Strike to Forehead: Execute a snapping strike to the front of the forehead causing whiplash. The rapid motion of the head causes hyperextension of the neck muscles and cervical vertebrae, and compression of the spinal nerve roots.

C. Strike to Throat: Clothesline an opponent at the throat. This variation often leads to a choke hold or a throw.

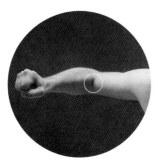
Inner Elbow

Back Elbow Strike to solar plexus

A. Inner Elbow Strike to back of skull-neck junction

B. Inner Elbow Strike to forehead causing whiplash

C. Inner Elbow Strike to throat

Leg strikes, commonly called kicks, are hitting techniques that use specific surfaces of the foot, lower leg, or knees for delivering blows anywhere on the body. Leg strikes can be executed while standing, jumping, flying through the air, falling, kneeling, or reclining on the ground. Some martial arts possess hundreds of different kicks, used in a wide range of situations, while others use a more limited repertoire, often restricted to very specific circumstances. Knowing many kicks does not necessarily imply superiority in combat, but it

LEG STRIKES

does allow you to respond to a broader range of combative situations, and to better understand the strengths and limitations of kicks being directed against you. This chapter outlines 86 leg strikes used in Hapkido, which are also found in other martial arts. The following pages provide an overview of basic principles and footwork, followed by a description of each leg strike, outlining their biomechanical qualities, appropriate uses, and relationships to each other. Typical self-defense applications can be found in subsequent chapters.

Overview

There are many different types of kicks, which use a variety of attack points and deliveries, for a wide range of purposes. Some kicks are used extensively; others only in specific circumstances. As kicking techniques become modernized over time in response to changes occurring throughout the martial arts world, the frequency and manner in which kicks are used also changes. Certain older kicks that were the foundation of many martial arts during the early to mid-twentieth century are less frequently used today, since more effective techniques or refinements have proven themselves over time.

In the martial arts world today, the art of kicking is evolving at a very rapid pace. Speed of execution, biomechanical efficiency, and tactics are radically different than they were even a decade ago. The differences between older and newer versions are most evident when comparing speed of delivery. Also the increased popularity and sophistication of grappling and throwing skills, used to counter kicks, has forced practical-oriented martial arts to reevaluate their kicking tactics.

The kick techniques illustrated in this chapter consist of both older and newer kicking techniques. When selecting kicks to address a specific need, be aware that every technique has a limited range of appropriate uses, and even this is constantly changing.

Types of Kicks

The kicks shown in this chapter are those commonly observed across a range of styles, and are organized into three categories:

- Standing Kicks
- Ground Kicks (drop and seated)
- Jump Kicks

Standing Kicks

Standing kicks are executed from standing postures while stationary or moving in any direction. They are used to hit targets anywhere on the body of standing, kneeling, or reclining opponents. Most martial arts prefer to execute standing kicks from strong, balanced postures. In Hapkido, kicks are also practiced from unbalanced postures, such as when falling or being thrown.

Ground Kicks

Ground kicks are very similar to standing kicks, except they are delivered from a kneeling, seated, or reclining position. Kicks are usually directed to standing opponents; however, kneeling or reclining targets are also possible. There are two types of ground kicks: *drop kicks* and *seated kicks*. Drop kicks are executed while making a transition from standing to ground positions, often returning to standing postures at the completion of the kick. They are also called *sacrifice kicks* or *falling kicks*. Seated kicks are executed from a kneeling, seated, or reclining position.

Jump Kicks

Jump kicks are executed while both feet are suspended above the ground, immediately following a jump or leap, or during a step (the kick occurs before the stepping foot touches down). The body may be directed straight upward or in any direction, depending upon the application. The height of the jump varies based on technique and objectives. In modern fighting, jump kicks are primarily used for: fast counterattacks, to span distance, or to chase down a retreating opponent.

Stylistic Qualities

Different martial arts will often articulate the same kick differently, or employ it in distinctly different circumstances. This is one of the reasons that the kicks of one martial art will be visually distinct from those of another. Nevertheless, the fundamental biomechanical actions of the kicks themselves are usually very similar, if not the same. The kicks in this book come from Hapkido and therefore exhibit characteristics associated with that art, as well as other Korean martial arts. Consequently, it may be necessary for you to modify certain aspects of the kicks shown, based on qualities associated with the martial style you practice. This can involve differences in: the use of your upper body; hand positions; the use of your hips; the use of your support foot (e.g., flat on the ground versus rising on the ball of the foot); the preferred kick-height (low versus high); the

Standing Kick

Ground Kick

Jump Kick

specific footwork used to set up a kick; and preferences for certain attack points (your hitting surfaces) and targets (what you hit).

Variations in Body Position

The position of the upper body, arms, and hands can vary based on the style you practice. In some styles, the head is often dropped low for protection, to make targeting difficult, to reduce strain on the lower back, and to increase power (particularly during spins) by centering the body's balance at the hips. In other styles, the head is usually held high to maintain a balanced, rooted stance, hinder kicks to the head, or promote speed. Likewise, the position of the hands can also vary. They can be used for blocking, held out to the sides for balance, or be touching the ground for support during high kicks.

Variations in Delivery

When observing a specific kick, one often sees very different deliveries being used by different martial artists. Is one better than another? This is often a matter of opinion. For example: In many styles, traditional Crescent Kicks, Hook Kicks, and Axe Kicks often use a straight-leg delivery for increased power, particularly when executed from a relaxed walking stance. Modern versions of the same kicks often use a bent-leg tuck, which changes to a straight-leg as the kick progresses (see page 96 and 98). This has been found to provide a faster delivery and more power, by using the inward-outward snap of the lower leg. The bent leg also better protects the groin area early in the delivery, and sets up for a variety of kicks, making it difficult for the defender to anticipate exactly which kick is coming. The delivery you use is entirely a matter of choice. Most can be very effective when used in appropriate situations.

Generating Power

The key factors influencing the force of a kick are muscle strength, leg velocity, and the manner in which you use your arms, upper body, support leg, and hips. All of these factors must be well-timed and coordinated based on the kick you are executing. In many kicks, the use of the hips can be particularly important and might involve either thrusting or rotational movements. Even during fast snap-kicks, the leg and hips can be momentarily extended through the target before retracting the leg. This leg and hip extension, which increases power, is usually more sensible in mid-level or low kicks, since the likelihood of having your leg caught is negligible. An example of pronounced hip extension is shown in the lower-left photo.

Attack Point Selection

Many kicks can be executed using different attack points (hitting surfaces). For example, a Front Kick can be executed using the ball of the foot, bottom of the heel, toe, instep, or edge of the foot. When selecting hitting surfaces, try to use the attack point that most efficiently damages the target. This is based on target size, shape, and the degree to which it is exposed or protected. For example, a Side Kick to the knee is more effective using a Knife Foot than a Bottom Heel. In this situation, the Knife Foot also requires less accuracy to be effective. In contrast, a Side Kick directed to the solar plexus might use the Bottom Heel, since the shape of this attack point matches the opening at the sternum (see below).

Use attack point which best corresponds to target.

Use of the Hands

During a kick, the position of the hands can be used to: influence your balance, add force to the strike, guard against counter attacks, or execute simultaneous blocks or strikes. The photos shown at right demonstrate typical hand positions used when kicking. A front kick is shown as a typical example, although these principles are applied to other kicks as well. From a practical standpoint, how the hands should be used is mostly a matter of individual style and tactics.

Kicking with low-hands for balance

Kicking with high-hands for protection

Kicking with simultaneous forearm block

Footwork

The footwork preceding a kick can be extremely important for: establishing distance, increasing speed and power, or avoiding and countering in a single movement. Various forms of footwork were previously covered in the *Fundamentals* chapter. These basic methods of stepping are combined with kicks in countless ways, leading to innumerable variations. Today, developments in kicking footwork are changing at a very rapid pace, with speed of execution and biomechanical efficiency being vastly improved from where they were even a decade ago. Particular steps are often used with specific kicks in very specific situations. Consequently, a qualified teacher is very important. Exceptionally efficient use of kicking footwork can be currently seen in Olympic-Style Taekwondo.

Ten basic methods of stepping used to initiate a kick are shown at right. In practical application many other forms of footwork are also used. The footwork shown provides excellent training for novices learning to coordinate basic movements and kicks, and should be practiced with all forms of standing kicks. Most of these examples are shown being applied from fighting stances. If you practice a self-defense martial art, all footwork should be practiced from relaxed stances as well (see 4).

1. No Step
Do not step. Kick with either leg. This is used when you are already in range of the target.

2. One Step
Take one step and kick in a single continuous motion with the rear leg. The step is used to move closer and generate power. Adjust the length of step based on target distance.

3. Two step
Take two steps and kick in a single continuous motion with the rear leg. The step is used to move closer from greater distances. Adjust the length of the step based on target distance. At closer distances, short steps can be used to effect a quick stance change, setting up a rear-leg attack (called a *stutter step*).

1. No Step

2. One Step

3. Two Step

4. Walking

5. Jump Step

6. *One-Foot Skip Step (hop on supporting leg during kick)*

7. *Two-Foot Hop Step (hop on both legs before kick)*

8. *Swing Step or Draw Step*

9. *Cross Step*

10. *Turn Step*

4. Walking

Walk forward in a relaxed manner and kick with the rear leg. Adjust your stride and number of steps based on target distance. This footwork is used to disguise your intent.

5. Jump Step

Jump steps can also be used to move forward or back, usually to chase an opponent down, retreat while countering, or increase speed of delivery by eliminating full steps. Step with one foot; spring off and kick with the other.

6. One-Foot Skip Step

As you kick, hop on the supporting leg during the delivery. This extends the kick's range and is useful if your opponent is fading away.

7. Two-Foot Hop Step

As you execute a kick, hop on both feet toward the opponent before kicking, to move within range. This is often used during a Turning Back Kick or Hook Kick when your opponent is fading away, or when you wish to keep both feet planted until the last possible moment (e.g., defending against a grappler).

8. Swing Step or Draw Step

In one continuous movement, swing the hips forward as the back foot slides to the front foot, and the front foot kicks. This step is used to generate power and close distance when using lead-leg kicks. *Hip swing* is often the key factor influencing speed.

9. Cross Step

The rear foot steps past the front foot, and the front foot kicks. This is used to create power and close distance for front-leg kicks. It covers greater distance than a *swing step*. Whether you step in front of, or behind, the lead leg depends on the kick: *behind* is used for Back Kicks and Hook Kicks; *in front* is used for Roundhouse Kicks and Inside Crescent Kicks. Side Kicks can use either.

10. Turn Step

In one continuous motion, pivot and turn toward the posterior side, kicking with the rear leg (often used for Back, Spin, or Hook Kicks).

FRONT KICKS

Front kicks are directed straight forward to any target, using one of four attack points: *Ball Foot* (greater reach), *Bottom Heel* (greater power), *Spear Foot* (pinpoint targeting), or *Instep Foot* (rising strikes). In Hapkido, the *Knife Foot* is also used, but this is not common to most arts. The specific attack point used depends upon target size and shape, and the method of delivery. In terms of the kick's delivery, there are three basic methods of executing a front kick: snapping, thrusting, and rising straight-leg. In *snap kicks,* the foot follows an upward circular path, with the knee acting as fulcrum as the hips thrust forward. The foot is quickly withdrawn. In *thrusting kicks,* the knee is extended as the toot follows a straight and sometimes downward path, usually while stepping

Ball Foot

Bottom Heel

Spear Foot and Instep Foot

Front Ball Kick to abdomen at CO-6

Front Heel Kick to underside of jaw

forward. In *rising kicks,* the straight leg is brought upward, with the hip-leg junction acting as fulcrum. The knee is not bent to prepare the kick, as it is in the first two methods described. Four typical front kicks are shown; many other possibilities exist.

1. Front Ball Kick

This is a snapping strike directed to targets anywhere on the body, using the Ball Foot. The foot follows an upward vertical circular path with the chambered knee initially pointing toward the target, as the lower leg snaps forward, assisted by a *forward thrust of the hips.* Quickly retract the leg to avoid being thrown, and to prepare for the next technique. The support leg is slightly flexed with the foot flat or raised onto the ball (increased reach). This kick is also applied using a Spear Foot to hit sensitive targets.

2. Front Heel Kick

Same as the previous kick, except you will strike with the Bottom Heel, targeting the belly, solar plexus, or underside of the chin.

3. Front Thrust Kick

This is a thrusting strike using the Bottom Heel or Ball Foot to hit targets such as the face, solar plexus, hip, thigh, or knee. When compared to the previous two kicks, this kick is delivered by *extending the knee,* as opposed to snapping the lower leg. Raise the leg as high as possible with the knee fully bent. When the sole faces the target, push the knee forward as you extend the foot. Use forward hip-thrust and body motion to create power, usually while stepping forward. The leg must be fully extended as you hit, to prevent the force of impact from unbalancing you backward. The kick works best when directed slightly downward to lower targets, since high kicks tend to upset your balance.

4. Rising Front Kick

The foot follows a rising circular path, with the leg extended. Power comes from the rising motion of the hips and a short snap of the knee. Use the Bottom Heel, Ball Foot, or Spear Foot. This kick can be used from relaxed stances, where it is well disguised and uses natural walking motions to initiate the kick. Slide the rear foot toward the front foot (*swing step*) to launch a front-leg kick.

Front Thrust Kick to solar plexus at CO-15

Rising Front Kick to SP-11, counters Side Kick

ROUNDHOUSE KICKS

Roundhouse kicks follow a circular path (horizontal or angular). Delivery is primarily characterized by the snapping of the lower leg, with the knee acting as a fulcrum. The kick may be executed using either the Instep Foot or Ball Foot to hit targets at any height, with either leg. The attack point used depends upon the target selected. Instep kicks are usually directed to the head, ribs, abdomen, hip, thigh, or knee. Ball Foot kicks are usually used to strike the kneecap, groin, solar plexus, neck, or jaw. Make sure the toes are curled back to prevent damage. When wearing shoes, the tip may be used instead. Roundhouse kicks can be used as finishing blows or to set up other techniques, frequently by striking low targets to lower the head. Roundhouse kicks have a high rate of accuracy.

5. Roundhouse Kick

This a snapping or thrusting strike in which the lower leg follows an inward circular path, pivoting at the knee. Raise the leg, pointing the knee directly at the target. Snap the lower leg forward as the support leg pivots 180°. This pivot turns the hips, which increases power and reach, and reduces twisting stress at the supporting knee. Immediately retract the foot to

Instep Foot

Ball Foot

Roundhouse Kick to groin (using Ball Foot option)

45° Roundhouse Kick to floating ribs

prepare for the next technique. Power comes from lower-leg velocity and hip-turn. If your kicks lack power, it may result from a slow delivery, insufficient pivot, or failing to project your foot through the target. Older styles of the roundhouse kick began with the chambered knee pointing to the side (rather than at the target). While the longer delivery and hip rotation results in more power, the kick is easily detected and countered. By modern standards, it is too slow to be practical except as a finishing blow. However, when teaching novices, the older style is often easier to learn initially.

6. 45° Roundhouse Kick

This is the same as the Roundhouse Kick (#5), only you deliver the blow at a 45° angle. It is used to hit the face or chest of a partially bent-over opponent, or to sneak under the guarding elbows to strike the ribs. In this situation, exercise caution: if your instep hits the point of the elbow, you will likely break your foot. Blocks using the elbow or shin are common counters.

7. Shin Roundhouse Kick

This is the same as the Roundhouse Kick (#5), only you strike with the bony front of the lower leg, using a snapping or circular thrusting delivery. This is often used at closer distances or when greater hitting power is required. Targets include the ribs, hip, thigh, knee, or lower leg.

8. Reverse Roundhouse Kick

The foot follows an outward circular path, the opposite of a normal roundhouse. This kick is used to strike an opponent standing in front, at your side, or slightly behind, using the instep or toes. While it is called a *roundhouse*, it is mechanically quite different. To execute, raise the leg with the bent-knee pointing slightly sideways. Snap the lower leg diagonally up and across, using a slight hip-turn to increase power and range of motion. The kick is often applied using a *cross step* to move closer, position the hips, and generate power. Although not a powerful kick, it can still provide a forceful shock by linking lower-leg speed with hip rotation. Power diminishes as height increases. Targets include the face, chest, hip, thigh, groin (use toes), and knee. It is also called a *Twist Kick, Lateral Kick,* or *Slap Kick.*

Shin Roundhouse Kick to nerve on thigh at GB-31

Reverse Roundhouse Kick to side of head

SIDE KICKS

Side kicks are powerful strikes directed to targets anywhere on the body, using either the Knife Foot, Bottom Heel, or the entire sole of the foot. They are usually directed to the side, but can also be used to strike in other directions by turning the hips and support leg during delivery. The foot follows a straight path with one exception (Rising Side Kick). The specific delivery and attack point used depends on the type of side kick employed and the profile of the target selected. Basic side kicks are:

9. Side Thrust Kick

This is a powerful straight thrusting strike using either the Knife Foot, Bottom Heel, or the entire sole for hitting. When using the Knife Foot, the ankle must be strong, well tensed and properly aligned to prevent it from collapsing (spraining) under the impact of a powerful strike. For this reason, the Bottom Heel or sole are often preferred, since the ankle is placed in a much stronger anatomical position. This is useful for individuals with weak or previously injured ankles. Experiment by striking a heavy bag to evaluate your technique and determine what works best for you. To execute a Side Thrust Kick, raise the leg with the knee fully bent. Thrust the foot

Knife Foot

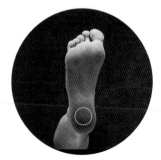

Bottom Heel

Side Thrust Kick to belly (using Bottom Heel option)

Side Snap Kick to lower leg (using Knife Foot)

straight out as the hips turn over and the supporting leg pivots 180° (support heel points to the target). This is crucial for power and reach. The leg is fully extended as your hip and body motion add force to the strike. Retract the foot along the same path. This kick is most powerful when the leg is at a 90° angle to the surface being hit. The face, midsection, and knees are common targets.

10. Side Snap Kick

This is a very fast, snapping strike using the Knife Foot to hit middle or low targets. It is often used like a Jab Punch to distract, set up a combination, or keep an opponent from moving closer. The Side Snap Kick is executed similarly to a Side Thrust Kick, except the supporting leg does not pivot, the hips are stationary, and the leg is retracted very quickly. The absence of these body movements reduces power and reach but greatly increases speed and recovery time. The kick is most effective when directed to sensitive points on the leg (GB-31, SP-10, SP-9, ST-34, SP-6). To dislocate the kneecap, hit 45° downward.

11. Rising Side Kick

The foot traces a rising circular path, with the leg extended throughout the delivery. This kick is used to strike the shin, knee-cap, or underside of an extended arm or leg (sometimes to break a hold). Traditionally it was also used to counter a Side Kick or Straight Punch by striking up to the knee or elbow of the striking-limb. However, the long delivery makes this impractical against modern strikes (which are quickly retracted), unless it is well set up, or the kicker's leg remains briefly extended.

12. Push Kick

This light, thrusting strike is used to feint, set up subsequent techniques, or to knock opponents off-balance. Raise one leg with the knee slightly bent, quickly pushing the sole into the opponent's hip while pivoting your support leg for greater reach. A *skip step* (hop on the support leg) is often used to close distance. Push Kicks can be used to jam a charging opponent, or counter a Back Kick or Spin Kick as an attacker turns (before the kick is launched). Push Kicks are often used to set up Back Kicks.

Rising Side Kick to back of elbow at TW-12   *Push Kick to hip, to counter a turning kick*

BACK KICKS

Back kicks are directed to targets behind you, hitting with the Bottom Heel. They can be executed using a snapping, thrusting, or rising circular delivery, depending on the specific kick employed. Back kicks can also be directed to opponents in front or to the side, when preceded by a turn step. Common targets include the solar plexus, abdomen, hip, thigh, groin, knee, and head. Back kicks are difficult to detect, and consequently hard to block or counter. Basic back kicks are:

13. Back Kick

This can be either a snapping or thrusting strike. Raise the knee and lean your upper body slightly forward, while keeping the leg fully bent. The kicking knee brushes the supporting knee as it passes backward. When the lower leg aligns with the target, extend the foot straight backward. You can either track the target by looking over your shoulder before kicking, or simply drop your head and strike (faster). Against multiple attackers, look straight ahead (not at the target). In snapping kicks, the foot is quickly retracted, with leg extension based on distance. In thrusting strikes, the knee is momentarily

Bottom Heel

Knife Foot

Back Kick to groin (while facing attacker in front)

Back Side Kick to abdomen or floating ribs

locked-out as you thrust through the target. Common errors are: not fully bending the kicking knee (loss of power), extending the leg too early (loss of accuracy and height), and leaning too far forward (loss of balance).

14. Back Side Kick

This is a *Side Thrust Kick* directed to the rear. The support leg and hips do not pivot, as they are already positioned. Look over your shoulder, bring the bent-leg out to the side (horizontal), and kick straight back, hitting the target using the Bottom Heel.

15. Uppercut Back Kick

The Bottom Heel snaps upward to the groin, midsection, or underside of the chin, similar to an Uppercut Punch. Do not chamber the leg, since this only slows delivery. Bring the foot directly upward, with the knee bent about 90° throughout the delivery. This kick is normally used at close range to sneak under the guard, or when space does not permit full extension.

16. Rising Back Kick

Sweep your extended-leg straight backward, using the Knife Foot or hard edge of your shoe to strike the shin or base of the kneecap. This kick is frequently used in combinations directed at multiple opponents. It is difficult to detect or block, and can be executed very quickly. The Rising Back Kick can also be easily applied from relaxed stances, where it is well disguised and can use natural walking motions to initiate the kick. Because the kick is low and your foot can be quickly returned to the ground, it is also useful in grappling situations in which higher kicks expose you to throws.

Uppercut Back Kick to solar plexus and chest

Rising Back Kick to base of kneecap

91

17. Rising Heel Kick

This is a fast, snapping strike using the Back Heel to hit upward to horizontal targets such as the groin, underside of an attacker's leg, or the chest and face of a bent-over opponent. It is useful for countering front or side thrust kicks, breaking a hold, and is indispensible in close-distance fighting. This kick is most effective when hitting targets located at a height between your knee and shoulder. To execute, bring the Back Heel rapidly upward by bending the knee. In the photos, the front foot slides toward the rear foot to launch a rear-foot kick. If desired, drop your head and shoulders to assist the kick. This also protects your head against high attacks. In certain situations (e.g., multiple attackers), it is

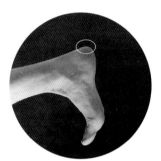

Back Heel

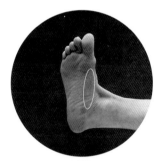

Arch Foot

Inner Heel

Rising Heel Kick to groin

Stamp Kick to neck at sternoceidomastoid muscle

prudent to keep your head high, to protect it from being kicked. Both versions are shown. Rising Heel Kicks are usually directed to the rear, but can also strike in other directions by turning the hips and support leg during delivery. The kick is often preceded by a step in any direction.

The Rising Heel Kick can also be executed using the Knife Foot (blade of your foot). The Knife Foot is often preferred when countering kicks, since its longer hitting surface is less likely to deflect off the underside of an attacker's leg.

18. Stamp Kick

This downward strike uses the Bottom Heel or sole to stomp on the knee, shin, instep, or toes (standing opponent), or anywhere on a reclining opponent. Raise the leg and stomp downward in any direction, shifting weight to the kicking leg if feasible. Stamp Kicks can be used to set up combinations, pin an opponent's foot, or escape holds such as a bear-hug from behind or a wrist-hold from front. You may also rake the lower leg as you stomp the foot.

19. Descending Arch Kick

This downward thrusting strike uses the Arch Foot or sole to hit the knee or leg, often to block a kick, counter a hip throw (see photo), or effect a takedown. The delivery is directed 45° downward, with the toes pointed outward. This technique requires good hip-turnout (flexibility in the hip-leg joint), making it difficult to execute for some individuals, particularly as the kick's height increases.

20. Shin Kick

This is a low, forward thrusting strike using the Inner Heel or inner edge of a shoe sole to hit the ankle or shin. The leg is initially bent, then snaps forward into the target, assisted by forward thrust of the hips. On impact the toes are curled back with the foot and ankle firmly tensed. This kick is normally used at closer distances. Power comes from lower leg velocity combined with hip thrust. The knee acts as a fulcrum, similar to a soccer kick. The kick can also be executed without cocking the lower leg, by sweeping the foot forward, close to the ground. This is also called a *Scoop Kick*.

Descending Arch Kick to back of knee (takedown)   *Shin Kick to nerves on lower leg, at SP-6 or KI-8*

21. Circular Inner-Heel Kick

This is a low, circular glancing strike using the Inner Heel to hit the knee, kneecap (dislocates laterally), inner shin (KI-8, SP-6, LV-5), or ankle. To execute, raise one leg with the knee bent. Snap the leg outward and across your body as your turning hips add force to the strike. Your kicking foot should be parallel to the ground with the toes leading the heel. This kick is usually used at closer distances.

22. Inside Hook Kick

This is an inward circular kick using the Back Heel to strike the ribs, hip, groin, thigh, knee, and lower leg. Raise and extend the leg out to the side. Pull the heel inward and down at a 45° angle by snapping the leg closed. Power comes from the rapid outward-inward snap of the lower leg. As you hook your leg inward, lean your head and upper body toward the kicking leg. This adds power to the kick and drops the head to avoid high strikes.

Inner Heel

Back Heel

Circular Inner-Heel Kick to kneecap

Inside Hook Kick to nerve on outer thigh at GB-31

94

23. Circular Blade Kick

This is a low, circular glancing strike using the Knife Foot or outer edge of the heel to hit the knee, shin, or ankle. To execute, raise one leg with the knee bent. Snap the foot forward and across your body as your turning hips add force to the strike. The foot travels parallel to the ground, tracing a long arc. The circular motion can be used to generate additional turning strikes (e.g., Spin Kick, turning Back Fist) or to hit the legs of multiple opponents with a single delivery. This kick is also called a *Grand Circular Kick*.

24. Reverse Circular Blade Kick

This is similar to the previous *Circular Blade Kick*, except the foot travels in the opposite direction. The kick is usually directed to the rear, but can also be used to strike to the side or front when preceded by a step. To execute, raise one leg with the knee partially bent. Snap the foot outward and across your body, tracing a long arc. This kick is also called a *Reverse Grand Circular Kick*.

Knife Foot

Circular Blade Kick to knee

Reverse Circular Blade Kick to inner knee

25. Inside Crescent Kick

This is a fast, circular kick traveling from the outside inward, using the Arch Foot or Inner Heel to strike or block. Targets include the head, midsection, spine, groin, or extended arm or leg. In a whipping motion, bring the leg up and outward, then rapidly inward across your body. The leg remains partially bent throughout—more at the start, less at impact. Hip rotation, leg whip, and lower-leg velocity are essential. For greater speed, keep the delivery within the width of your shoulders. In some styles, the leg is not initially bent, but is extended throughout the delivery. Crescent kicks are also called *Full-Moon Kicks* or *Wheel Kicks*.

26. Outside Crescent Kick

This is a fast, circular strike traveling from the inside outward, using the Knife Foot or outer-edge of the heel to strike or block targets at waist-height or higher. The kick is similar to an Inside Crescent Kick, only the foot follows the opposite path. In a whipping motion, bring the leg inward across your body, then rapidly outward into the target. The leg can be bent or extended as outlined in kick 25. Since crescent kicks are not powerful, speed is crucial. You can also use a Cutting Foot (toenails or the edge of a shoe) to slash the eyes or face.

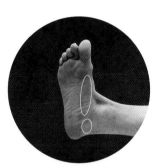

Arch Foot and Inner Heel

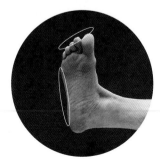

Knife Foot and Cutting Foot

Inside Crescent Kick to jaw and side of head

Outside Crescent Kick to jaw and side of head

27–28 Axe Kicks

The Axe Kick is a devastating downward blow directed to a standing, bent-over or reclining opponent. Strike using one of three attack points: *Back Heel* (greater power), *Ball Foot* (greater reach), or *Knife Foot* with foot extended (pinpoint targeting). Regardless of which attack point you use, two basic deliveries are used for all Axe Kicks: outside or inside. An *Outside Axe Kick* begins like an Outside Crescent Kick. It is usually preferred since the rising leg protects the groin and other frontal targets, should an opponent counter early in the delivery. An *Inside Axe Kick* begins like an Inside Crescent Kick. It is often used at close range or when an outside delivery isn't practical. In both deliveries, the foot is raised as high as possible, then slammed downward into the target. Power comes from leg speed (fast up, very fast down), and the contraction of hamstring muscles reacting against the high foot position. Keep the knee slightly flexed to prevent hyper-extension at impact. The lower the target, the more powerful the kick. Axe Kicks can be used to initiate an attack, counter a charge (attacker runs into kick), attack an extended kick, or finish-off a bent-over or reclining opponent. Targets include the chest, shoulder, spine, head, and limbs.

Back Heel

Ball Foot

Axe Kick to collarbone (using Knife Foot option)

Axe Kick to cervical spine (using Back Heel option)

29. Hook Kick

This is an outward circular strike directed to the front, side, or rear, using the Back Heel to hit any target at any height. Raise and extend the leg out to the side. Pull your heel outward and across your body, toward the target. Rapidly bend the knee at impact to add force to the blow. Some stylists pull the upper body back away from the kick to add force to the strike. Targets include the head, torso, spine, kidneys, hip, thigh, knee, and lower leg. This kick can be deceptive when hitting an opponent's closed (blind) side at close range, and is often used to hook around the guard.

30. Spin Kick

The Spin Kick is one of the hallmarks of Hapkido and other Korean martial arts. This devastating circular strike uses the Back Heel to hit targets at any height. The kick is always preceded by a turn step to develop the spinning motion from which the kick derives its power. The entire body rotates 360°, adding force to the strike. Spin Kicks must be very fast, since slower deliveries are easily avoided or countered. The key to speed is staying *very relaxed* and concentrating on *hip rotation*. The hips and shoulders always precede the foot. Targets include the temple, jaw, face, neck, spine, ribs, leg, and knee. The analogy of "swinging a rock tied to the end of a rope" is often used to characterize the explosive power of this kick.

Back Heel

Hook Kick (modern bent-leg delivery, using a cross step)

Hook Kick (traditional straight-leg delivery)

Executing a Basic Spin Kick

1. Initiate a turn step using either your front or back leg, depending on target distance. To develop adequate rotational force, make sure to step past an imaginary line connecting your body and the target. Once you step, don't stop spinning until the kick is finished, returning the kicking foot to the rear position.

2. As you begin to turn back toward your opponent, look at the target from under or around your shoulder, as you bend at the waist.

3. Raise your leg. Allow your hip and upper body rotation to propel your foot inward while rotating on the ball of the supporting foot. The kicking leg is straight and travels parallel to ground, tracing a 360° arc. Your head position can vary from waist-level to the higher level shown in the third photo.

Different martial arts articulate the head position differently. Generally, a lower head position is what differentiates Hapkido spin kicks from those of other styles such as Taekwondo or Kung Fu. Kicks with the head high might be slightly faster; kicks with the head low are more powerful. This power is likely produced by increased rotational force resulting from the opposing positions of the head and leg. Modern stylists are also executing Spin Kicks that cut slightly upward (rather than horizontal) to more effectively target the jaw. Spin kicks from the ground or a jump are covered later in this chapter.

31. Hook Spin Kick

This is similar to a Spin Kick, except the leg is bent during early delivery, then straightens at impact. Snap the leg partially closed as you hit through the target, to add force to the blow.

Spin Kick

Hook Spin Kick

Knee strikes are devastating thrusting kicks using the *Front Knee* attack point to hit targets anywhere on the body. Like elbow strikes, they are normally used at close range and are very effective at creating space when you are being held or crowded. They are particularly useful against grapplers. In most Hapkido knee strikes, the foot is fully extended (toes pointing) and the knee fully bent throughout the delivery. The "pointing of the toes" is believed to increase power, although many other martial arts styles point the heel instead (foot fully bent) for the same reasons. Keeping the leg fully bent tightens and protects the various parts of the knee which are so easily damaged. Even so, knee strikes are safest when directed to softer targets. When striking hard surfaces such as the head, modify power accordingly. Individuals with chronic or permanent knee injuries should not use these techniques.

1. Rising Knee Strike

This is an upward thrusting strike directed to the head of a bent-over opponent. It is normally used as a finishing blow. Grasp the opponent's head, with your fingers wrapping around to the back of the skull. Pull the head downward as you drive your knee upward into the face, side or back of head. If the opponent is properly positioned, this technique can also be used to attack the spine, sternum, solar plexus, or the knee of a held leg (typically when countering a kick; shown in *Defense Against Kicks* chapter).

Front Knee

Rising Knee Strike to face (pull head into knee)

Front Knee Strike to solar plexus

2. Front Knee Strike

This is a straight thrusting strike directed to mid-height targets. To execute, point the knee directly at the target. Thrust the hips forward, similar to a front kick, using your hands to pull the opponent into the strike if possible. Maintain balance by leaning your upper body backwards. The supporting foot may be flat or raised onto the ball, depending upon target height and distance. Common targets include the torso, ribs, kidneys, and groin.

3. Roundhouse Knee Strike

This is similar to a traditional Roundhouse Kick, except you are striking with the knee, to mid-height targets. The knee follows a horizontal circular path or cuts upward at a 45° angle. To execute, push off with the kicking leg, to elevate the knee and generate the necessary hip rotation. As the hips turn toward the target, rotate the shoulders in the opposite direction of the hips, pulling the knee into the target. These opposing motions of the hips and shoulders help maintain balance and add force to the strike. When possible, body rotation is assisted by grabbing and pulling the opponent into the strike. Targets include the chest, spine, ribs, kidneys, abdomen, hip, thigh, and groin.

4. Side Knee Strike

This is similar to a Side Thrust Kick, except the lower leg is not extended. Strike with the knee or bony area directly below the kneecap. Forward momentum, hip rotation, and supporting-leg pivot (foot pivots 180°) are very important for both power and reach, since the delivery is very short. The most common targets are the front or outside of the upper leg (GB-31), or the lower-rear skull of a bent-over opponent. Sometimes the hip, lower spine, ribs, kidneys, and knee are also appropriate targets. Side Knee Strikes are frequently used to break a bent-arm choke, initiate a surprise strike by charging forward, drive a close opponent backwards, or distract an opponent before launching attacks to the upper body.

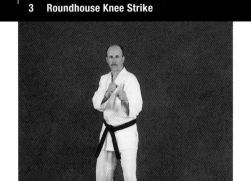

Roundhouse Knee Strike to floating ribs

Side Knee Strike to hip-leg junction

DROP KICKS

Drop kicks are very similar to standing kicks, except they are delivered from a crouching, kneeling, or reclining position, after transition from a standing posture. Upon completing the kick, you may either return to a standing posture or remain on the ground. Drop kicks can be directed to standing, kneeling, or reclining opponents. When attacking standing opponents, there is always an element of risk. If your strike is ineffective or your opponent avoids the kick, you are left in a vulnerable position (you are on the ground, they are standing). For this reason, drop kicks are usually used: when standing skills fail; as an unexpected surprise; while falling; or to take your opponent to the ground where you believe you possess an advantage. Whenever possible, execute a preliminary feint to disguise your kick. This might involve looking high, standing tall, throwing a high strike, etc. Generally, drop kicks should be very fast, continuous, and end in a standing posture.

Planted Knee vs Elevated Knee
When executing most drop kicks from crouching or kneeling positions (see kick 2), there are two methods of supporting your body. In the first method, the knee and ball of the foot are planted. In the second method, the ball of the foot is planted, with the knee elevated above the ground. Generally, a particular martial art will prefer one method over the other. Both have advantages and disadvantages best grasped by experimentation. Drop kicks in which the knee is planted are usually easier for beginners to learn.

Movement Preceding the Kick
Drop kicks begin from a standing posture and transition to the ground by one of three methods: 1) attacking footwork, 2) defending footwork, or 3) a ground-entry technique such as a sit-out or roll.

1. Attacking footwork involves moving toward the opponent, usually to seize the initiative. The type of step used depends upon the kick to be executed (e.g., a forward step for a front kick, a cross step for a side kick). The step can also be used as a feint or to avoid an attack.

2. Retreating footwork involves moving away from the opponent, usually to counter a charge or diminish the power of an incoming attack, particularly against an overpowering opponent. Retreating footwork is usually executed by performing the opposite steps you would use for moving forward.

3. A ground-entry technique is used when you wish to remain on the ground or are in the process of falling or running backwards. Ground-entry techniques are specific methods by which you transition to a kneeling or seated guard, prior to kicking. A sit-out entry (sitting down backwards onto your back) or a shoulder roll are the most common methods.

Since there are many footwork and ground-entry variations, only the most common methods are shown in the examples. The particular type of footwork depicted (attacking, retreating) is labeled below the last photo in each series, at the bottom of the pages. Drop kicks using ground-entry techniques are not shown in this text, but can be found in the author's books *Hapkido: Traditions, Philosophy, Technique* and *The Art of Ground Fighting*.

Returning to a Standing Posture
Many drop kicks are designed to permit rapid return to standing postures, in order to reduce the element of risk when confronting standing opponents. This is accomplished by using the fingertips of both hands and the ball of the foot for support. To return to a standing posture, simply push off with both hands and your supporting foot.

1. Drop Front Kick

Whether you attack or retreat, the technique is the same; only the footwork preceding it differs. To attack, the rear foot steps forward. To retreat, the front foot steps back. After the step, shift balance to the rear leg, planting the rear hand on the ground (front hand guarding). As you reach back to plant the other hand, execute a Front Ball Kick or Front Heel Kick with either leg. Raise the hips forward to assist the kick. Targets include the knee, groin, ribs, solar plexus, chin, and head.

Footwork used for attacking or retreating

2. Drop Roundhouse Kick

Front or rear leg strikes are possible, based on the preceding steps. To attack, step forward (straight or 45°), or drop directly to the ground. Plant both hands, lower the front knee, and execute a rear-leg kick (see photos). To retreat, the front foot steps to the rear. Lower the rear knee, plant both hands, and execute a front-leg kick (not shown). Targets include the knee, groin, solar plexus, and head.

3. Drop Side Kick

This kick is often executed from a Side Stance. It is powerful, versatile, and assists rapid return to a standing posture. It is safe to execute in a variety of situations, since the groin and frontal targets are well protected.

Whether you attack or retreat, the technique is the same; only the footwork preceding it differs. To attack, cross-step forward (rear foot passes behind front foot). During the cross step, plant both hands on the ground, lower the knee, and cock the opposite leg. Then deliver a Side Thrust Kick. To retreat, cross-step backward (front foot passes in front of rear foot), plant both hands, lower the rear knee, cock the opposite leg, and kick. Targets include the ankle, knee, groin, midsection, neck, and head. The kick may also be directed to the underside of an attacker's leg to counter a Side Kick.

Footwork used for attacking   *Footwork used for attacking or retreating*

4. Drop Back Kick

This kick is directed to an opponent behind. To attack, the front foot steps backward past the rear foot (toward opponent). To retreat, the rear foot steps forward past the front foot (away from opponent). While looking over your shoulder at the target, plant both hands and lower the knee of the stepping-foot. Cock the opposite leg and deliver a back kick. Place your chest close to the ground for higher kicks. Targets include the shin, knee, groin, midsection, throat, or the head if an opponent is bent over.

5. Drop Axe Kick

This kick is directed to an opponent in front. Execute an Axe Kick with the Bottom Heel, as you exit a forward shoulder roll. The rolling motion powers the kick, as your forward momentum propels you to a kneeling or standing position afterwards. Depending upon how the shoulder roll is executed, the kick can be used to strike targets at a variety of distances. Since the shoulder roll complicates timing and distance, this kick requires extensive practice to develop accuracy. If you do miss, continue to execute hand strikes as you move upward into the opponent, assuming a standing posture. This kick is rarely used but can be very effective in specific circumstances. Targets include the abdomen, groin, thigh, knee, toes, top of the foot, or anywhere on an opponent who is reclining on their back.

6. Drop Hook Kick

This kick normally uses the same attacking or retreating footwork as the Drop Side Kick. Drop Hook Kicks are usually directed to the side or back of the knees, to force a fall. You may also strike to the side of the head if an opponent is leaning over, or to the groin if an opponent is in a side stance. Because the Hook Kick is not inherently powerful, its effectiveness is usually maximized by striking sensitive points, particularly on the leg. Common targets include: SP-6 (inner shin); SP-9, SP-10 and ST-34 (knee area); SP-11 (inner thigh); GB-31 (outer thigh); LV-12 and SP-12 (cluster at hip-leg junction); and the testicles. Strikes to these pressure points usually weaken or buckle the legs.

Footwork used for attacking opponent behind you

Footwork used for attacking

7. Drop Spin Kick

This is a devastating kick to the knee, shin, or ankle. It is used to knock an opponent to the ground by upsetting the balance or damaging the lower leg. Pressure point targets are outlined in the previous kick. Like standing versions, very fast Drop Spin Kicks are a hallmark of Hapkido. There are two basic ways to execute a Drop Spin Kick: *foot pivot* and *knee pivot*. In the first method, the supporting leg is fully bent as you pivot on the ball of the foot. In the second method, the knee is planted and serves as pivot-point. The first method (foot pivot) is arguably faster, more powerful and permits rapid return to a standing position. The second method (knee pivot) is easier to execute, permits greater height (hit to the groin or upper leg), and can be used by individuals who cannot fully bend the knee due to previous injuries. In order to execute these kicks safely, you will need healthy knees with strong supporting musculature and tight ligaments.

Drop Spin Kick (foot pivot)

This kick is used to strike targets at knee height or lower. The technique is very similar to a standing Spin Kick, except the supporting leg is fully bent at the knee. As you step across to initiate the spin, lower yourself *straight down* to the ground. If you lean forward or backward as you drop, you will upset your balance during the spin. When first learning, plant both hands for support (fingertips, not palms). Later, the hands only touch lightly to stabilize your balance, or not at all. The key to speed and fluidity is staying relaxed and focusing on hip rotation. Do not allow the hips to rise. If you miss the target, continue spinning to a standing posture by rising on the support-ing leg, as you set the kicking leg down to the rear. The entire kick (stand-drop-stand) is applied in a very fast, continuous motion.

Drop Spin Kick (knee pivot)

The hand plant is used for balance and power. Rotate on the lower knee (not the kneecap), with the supporting foot lightly brushing against the ground. The hands push forward near the end of delivery to assist the spinning motion. To return to a standing posture, push off with your hands and supporting leg, like other drop kicks.

Footwork used for attacking or retreating

Footwork used for attacking (Spin Kick with foot pivot)

DROP TWIN KICKS

Drop twin kicks are ground strikes in which you simultaneously kick with both legs. The kicks are directed to either the same or to two different targets. These kicks can be practical in certain circumstances, such as: defending against multiple attackers, driving back an overpowering attacker (extra power needed), or fighting when your feet are tied together. Twin drop kicks are executed with the hips planted or airborne, based on your entry method. You will often use the same footwork and ground-entry methods as single-leg drop kicks.

When both feet and hips are airborne, the most difficult part of the kick is landing. You may land on either the balls of the feet or side of body. When landing on the balls of the feet, it is possible to quickly return to standing postures. In comparison, body landings can be fairly jarring, and should not be used until you are proficient in breakfalls. Remember, landing on a padded mat is very different than landing on concrete or asphalt. Twin kicks are also executed from a seated posture or jump (shown later in this chapter).

8. Drop Twin Front Kick

Execute two front kicks at the same time, with both feet very close together, buttocks planted on the ground. Either snapping or thrusting deliveries are possible. Strike with the Bottom Heel or Ball Foot. Use the attacking or retreating entries previously discussed (see Drop Front Kick). Thrusting deliveries can be used to drive a converging opponent or grappler backward.

9. Drop Twin Roundhouse Kick

Execute a two-foot Roundhouse Kick with both feet close together, using either the Instep or Ball Foot. When using attacking or retreating footwork, the entire body is airborne, with both hands planted and supporting. Land on the balls of the feet or side of the body. When using a sit-out entry (see kick 12), the hips and side of the torso are planted during the kick, with the hands maintaining a guard. Power comes from lower-leg speed and use of the abdominal muscles as you bend at the waist.

10. Drop Twin Side Kick

Execute a two-foot Side Kick with both feet very close together. When using attacking or retreating footwork, the body is airborne, with both hands planted and supporting. The entire body travels in the direction of the kick, to add force to the strike. If you fail to use body momentum, you may be knocked off-balance by the force of impact. Land on the balls of the feet or side of the body. The force of impact can be used to assist returning to a standing position. When using a sit-out entry (see kick 12), the hips and side of the torso are planted during the kick, with the hands maintaining a guard.

11. Drop Twin Back Kick

When compared to other twin kicks, this technique is quite powerful and fairly easy to perform. Execute a two-foot Back Kick with both feet very close together. Regardless of footwork, the body is always airborne, with both hands planted and supporting. The entire body travels in the direction of the kick, to add force to the strike. Land on both feet, returning to a standing posture. Use the attacking or retreating footwork shown for the Drop Back Kick. Sit-out entries are impractical.

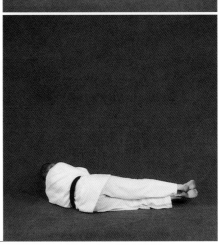

12. Drop Twin Overhead Kick

This kick is directed to an opponent behind, as you sit-out or fall backward. Its primary use is against two attackers standing in front and behind. As the front attacker pushes or throws you backward, execute a sit-out, using the rolling motion to deliver a Twin Front Kick to the rear attacker. Strike using the Ball Foot or the hard tips of your shoes. Grasp the attacker's ankles to increase power and keep them from stepping backward, which forces a fall to their rear.

13. Drop Front Split Kick

This kick is directed to two opponents standing in front, at your left and right sides. As you sit-out or fall backward, pull both feet together toward your buttocks with the knees fully bent. Angle your knees outward, pointing at both targets. Simultaneously snap both lower legs outward to either side, hitting with the Ball Foot or Bottom Heel. Immediately retract your feet, assuming a seated guard or continuing to other techniques. Common targets are the groin, knee, or shin.

14. Drop Side Split Kick

This twin kick is directed to two opponents standing in front, at your left and right sides. To execute, rotate your body so that one side is facing the ground. The top leg executes a side kick (Bottom Heel), while the bottom leg executes a front kick (Ball Foot or Bottom Heel). This is a difficult kick requiring good flexibility and much practice. When using attacking or retreating footwork, the entire body is airborne, with both hands planted and supporting. Land on your feet or the side of the body. When using a sit-out entry (see previous kick), the side of one hip is planted during the kick, with your hands maintaining a guard. In this situation, it is possible to execute multiple Side Split Kicks, in repetition. Targets include the thigh, knee, shin, or ankle. This kick is also commonly called a *Scissor Kick*.

15. Drop Overhead Split Kick

This is basically a *Side Split Kick* executed with your body resting on the upper back or shoulders. The kick is directed to two opponents standing in front and behind. As you sit-out or fall backward, execute the twin kicks. It is usually executed in continuous repetition, or linked with other ground kicks and takedowns. Depending on target and distance, hit with the Ball Foot, sole, or Back Heel. Targets include the groin, ribs, abdomen, and solar plexus.

SEATED KICKS

Seated kicks are very similar to standing kicks and drop kicks, except they are executed from a seated guard, relaxed seated posture, or during ground movement. Various forms of ground movement are outlined in the author's books *Hapkido: Traditions, Philosophy, Technique* and *The Art of Ground Fighting.*

Seated kicks are used for ground fighting against either standing or reclining opponents. They can be used to: take an opponent to the ground, defend against an unexpected attack while relaxing, attack grapplers during ground fighting, or keep attackers at a distance until you can recover a standing posture. Since seated kicks are basically the same as standing kicks, or drop kicks using a sit-out entry, entire sequences will not be shown. The seated kicks shown are among those most commonly used in martial arts with extensive ground-kicking repertories, such as Hapkido. However, almost any standing kick can be modified for use from ground positions. Experimentation is suggested.

16. *Seated Front Kick (to underside of chin)*

17. *Seated Front Blade Kick (to groin)*

18. *Seated Front Toe Kick (to throat, CO-22)*

19. *Seated Roundhouse Kick (ball foot to SP-10)*

20. *Seated Reverse Roundhouse Kick (to head)*

21. *Seated Side Kick (to knee, with leg trap at ankle)*

22. *Seated Back Kick (from side roll, to throat)*

23. *Seated Stamp Kick (to top of foot, LV-3)*

24. *Seated Circular Inner-Heel Kick (to kneecap)*

25. *Seated Inside Crescent Kick (to side of head)*

26. Seated Outside Crescent Kick (blocking knife)

27. Seated Cutting Crescent Kick (slashing the eyes)

28. Seated Axe Kick (to nose and cheekbone)

29. Seated Inside Hook Kick (to kneecap)

30. Seated Hook Kick (to knee, with leg trap at ankle)

31. Seated Twin Front Kick (to base of rib cage)

32. Seated Twin Roundhouse Kick (ball foot to groin)

33. Seated Twin Side Kick (to floating ribs)

34. Seated Twin Overhead Kick (to throat)

35. Seated Front Split Kick (to both inner knees)

36. Seated Side Split Kick (to both ankles, takedown)

37. Seated Overhead Split Kick (to both groins)

JUMP KICKS

Jump kicks are very similar to standing kicks, except they are executed while airborne, with both feet suspended above the ground. They are normally used to:

- Increase height or span greater distance
- Generate momentum and power
- Leap over an obstacle
- Crash through a ring of attackers
- Increase speed of attacks, counters, or combinations by stepping and kicking simultaneously, before the step is planted.

Any standing kick can become a jump kick, although some are more practical than others. Jump kicks are often used to: knock an opponent off-balance, add power to kicks against an overwhelming attacker (where a normal kick might be ineffective), strike multiple opponents simultaneously (called twin kicks), launch a kick while running away or chasing down an opponent, or attack while changing elevations, leaping off a stairway or platform or jumping over an obstacle.

Jump kicks can cover different distances and heights, depending on the situation and the method of jumping. They are usually directed horizontally or downward and basically use the same motions found in standing kicks. Although jump kicks are commonly directed to targets above the waist, any height can be effective, such as a Jump Side Kick to the kneecap. The jump itself is used to propel the body forward, backward, straight up, or in any other direction required. When executed from a running start, jump kicks add considerable force to a strike, since the weight of the entire body is behind the kick. Jump kicks that span greater distances are called *flying kicks.*

Jumping Methods

Three basic forms of jumping are used to begin most jump kicks. They may be executed while stationary, or used to create movement in any direction. This may involve no step, one step, two steps, or a full run. Three common methods are described below and shown at left. Some of these methods

were also shown at the beginning of this chapter under *Footwork.* Be aware that all jump methods may need to be modified based on a particular kick or what method works best for you.

Method 1

Raise one leg (lead or rear) with the knee bent; spring off and kick with the opposite leg. The kicking leg leaves the ground last. The jump is highly variable and can be used to hit close targets, or span greater distances. A lead Side Kick, rear Roundhouse Kick, or Turning Back Kick are typical examples.

Method 2

Raise the kicking leg first (knee bent); spring off with the opposite leg. This method is a more pronounced version of the One-Foot Skip Step covered at the beginning of this chapter under *Footwork.* It is often used to execute lead-leg kicks, execute the first kick in a two-kick jump combination, or extend the range of a standing rear-leg kick when an opponent is moving away. Side kicks, back kicks, and combination kicks (front–front, front–roundhouse, front–side) are common uses. It is also used in some turning kicks.

Method 3

Spring off both legs simultaneously; kick with either one or both legs. This method is used to move in any direction or return to a similar position. It is also used to deliver twin kicks (striking with both legs simultaneously).

Practical Considerations

In past decades, when opponents fought from low-mobility or wide stances, high jump kicks with long air-time were more popular. Today high jump kicks are generally felt to be impractical except in specific circumstances. This is because they are slow to develop and are easily countered, since an opponent has ample time to avoid and counterattack before you land. It should be remembered that in any kick, you are most vulnerable during the time it takes you to lift your leg, kick, and place the leg down. Once the leg is down, you can move, reposition, resume the attack, move

away, etc. Until then you remain vulnerable; the longer your jump kick remains in the air, the more vulnerable you become. This is particularly true against grapplers, who are watchful for any opportunity to upset your balance and bring the fight to the ground.

Jump Kicks with Long Air-Time

Since high, long-duration kicks are inherently risky, they are usually only appropriate when set up by feints or other preparatory techniques, in the following circumstances:

- Footing is secure (no loose gravel)
- A safe landing is assured
- Opponent is slow, or lacks mobility
- Opponent is trapped by obstacles
- Opponent is stunned and stationary
- Greater power is needed against an overwhelming attacker, risk is justified

Jump Kicks with Short Air-Time

In modern fighting, jump kicks are primarily used for fast attacks, counters, or combinations, in which you step and kick almost simultaneously. In these instances, the support foot barely leaves the ground. Speed of execution and jump direction are far more important than height, since the jump itself is used to avoid an attack or adjust to target distance. For example, an opponent steps forward and executes a mid-level roundhouse kick with the rear leg. If you remain stationary you will be hit. A typical non-jumping counter involves a step back (front foot slides toward rear foot, rear foot slides back), followed by a rear-leg roundhouse kick to the midsection. Using a jump kick, this entire process can be accelerated by beginning the rear-leg kick while the front foot is still in the air, leaving your opponent much less time to react.

Learning Jump Kicks

Jump kicks require excellent coordination, flexibility, and a good teacher, but can be mastered by most people willing to work at it. Before beginning, you must be proficient in standing kicks executed from various forms of movement, including stepping, sliding, skipping, and hopping. In twin jump kicks, the most difficult part is often the landing. For this reason you must also master the various forms of falling covered in the *Fundamentals* chapter under *Breakfalls*. When teaching jump kicks, most instructors concentrate initially on jumping and landing skills, independent of the kicks themselves. Trampolines and wall-bars are often used to increase jump height, allowing one more time to perfect motions. Complex twin kicks are best practiced on the ground first (shown previously under *Ground Kicks*), where it is easier to perfect body movements before combining them with jumps. The following suggestions should prove helpful when learning and applying most jump kicks:

• Drive the knees upward to gain additional height, as you spring off.

• While airborne, keep both legs bent and drawn up tightly under the body before kicking. This facilitates a more explosive kick, better balance, and greater protection should an opponent counter while you are airborne. After kicking, quickly retract both legs under the body to prepare for landing.

• Keep the torso upright or leaning toward the kick. Leaning back will upset your balance and reduce power. Land on the balls of the feet, flexing the knees and ankles to absorb shock and prepare for the next movement.

Jumping Methods

Method 1: Raise one leg, spring off and kick with opposite leg. Kicking leg leaves the ground last.

Method 2: Raise kicking leg, spring off with opposite leg. Kicking leg leaves the ground first.

Method 3: Spring off with both legs simultaneously, kick with either one or both legs.

1. Jump Front Kick

This is a snapping or thrusting strike using any standing front kick described previously. It is most powerful when directed forward rather than upward. The Ball Foot or Bottom Heel are the most common attack points and are usually directed to the solar plexus, face, or underside of the chin. Two jump front kicks can be combined into a single jump. Use any of the jump methods described on the previous page.

2. Jump Roundhouse Kick

Jump Roundhouse Kicks are very versatile and can be used for either attacking or countering. They are one of the fastest methods of countering a kick, and are normally directed to the midsection or knees in self-defense applications. Jump Roundhouse Kicks to the head are often used in low-high combinations, such as a Shin Kick to the leg, followed by a Jump Roundhouse Kick to the head.

3. Jump Side Kick

These kicks are most practical when used to unbalance an opponent by striking the waist, midsection, or knee. The kick is usually directed horizontally or downward. Kicking targets higher than the level of your airborne hips is discouraged, since upward kicks lose power, compromise your balance and make landing difficult. Head strikes ideally require very high jumps in order to place your hips at the same level as the target. This is usually impractical and very vulnerable to counters, since you are airborne awhile.

4. Jump Back Kick

Jump Back Kicks are commonly used for countering, or striking a charging opponent while retreating. The leg may be extended straight back to the midsection, or remain bent as it hooks upward in an uppercut motion to the groin, midsection, or head (see *Uppercut Back Kick* under *Standing Kicks*). Remember, back kicks by nature become highly unstable as you lower the head. In standing versions this can be overcome by briefly planting the hands for stability. In jump kicks this is not possible, therefore keep the upper body fairly erect as shown in the photos.

Ball Foot

Bottom Heel

Instep Foot

Knife Foot

1. Jump Front Kick

2. Jump Roundhouse Kick

3. Jump Side Kick

4. Jump Back Kick

5. Jump Turning Back Kick

Jump Back Kicks executed with the rear leg, or involving 180° of body rotation while airborne, are commonly called *turning* kicks. There are several different methods of jumping. The method shown in the photos is identical to the jump method described under *Jump Spin Kicks* (see *Executing the Kick*, next column). When comparing the two kicks, turning back kicks are more direct, more difficult to block, and require less skill to execute. The turning motion is often used to avoid an attack (by turning away), while simultaneously executing a counterattack. Practice standing versions first, to perfect your turn. Gradually shorten the time between stepping and kicking until it becomes a single movement.

6. Jump Axe Kick

Jump Axe Kicks can be executed with either leg, using any jump method. The jump shown in the photos is applied by raising the left leg, then springing off and kicking with the right leg. Swing the right leg as high as possible before slamming the Back Heel or Ball Foot downward into the target. This kick is usually used as a finishing blow, or for a surprise attack to the face or collarbone.

7. Jump Hook Kick

This is usually a front-leg kick using either one or both legs to spring off. It is often used to counter an attack while jumping backward, using the front leg to push back and the rear leg to spring upward and backward. Common targets are the head and knees.

8. Jump Spin Kick

There are numerous types of Jump Spin Kicks, which are primarily distinguished by the method of jumping, and the amount of rotation in the air (usually between 180° and 360°). These explosive, powerful kicks are widely practiced in Korean martial arts, particularly Hapkido and Taekwondo. Jump Spin Kicks are very similar to the standing versions on which they are based, except body rotation and the kick occur entirely in the air. This requires good timing, height, and strong rotational force to assure the kick has adequate power. Jump spin kicks which lack power usually result from underdeveloped body rotation. The following factors should always be considered:

- The springing and pushing actions of the legs are crucial to generating rotation.

- The head, shoulders, and hips always *lead* the kick, otherwise power is lost.

- Do not allow the head to drop too low, as this may unbalance your landing.

- Practice against a heavy bag as well as light targets, so you will understand how your balance is affected by impact.

Executing the Kick

To jump straight up or forward: shift your balance to the front leg while lowering the body by flexing both knees. Jump and spin by using the front leg to generate height (push straight up) and the rear leg to generate rotation (push forward). Note that although both feet leave the ground almost at the same time, they are *not* weighted equally. This kick may also be executed while jumping backwards, by reversing the roles of the jumping and pushing legs (shift balance to back leg, back leg springs up and kicks, front leg generates rotation). This kick requires about 180° of body rotation while in the air. Other common methods of jumping to deliver a Jump Spin Kicks are covered in the author's book *Hapkido: Traditions, Philosophy, Technique.*

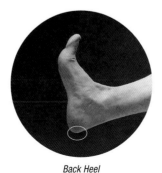

Back Heel

5. Jump Turning Back Kick

6. Jump Axe Kick

7. Jump Hook Kick

8. Jump Spin Kick

JUMP TWIN KICKS

These kicks strike one or two targets with both feet simultaneously, using the basic mechanics covered earlier in this chapter under *Ground Kicks*. Twin kicks require exceptional jumping ability and body control, making them very difficult to learn and execute. The landing is the most dangerous part, since you can easily turn an ankle, break your foot, or separate a shoulder from a bad fall. Therefore, it is vital that you learn proper breakfalls before practicing these kicks. When twin kicks are executed on the ground, or hands are used for support, these kicks can become more practical and easier to execute safely (see examples two pages later). Twin kicks would normally only be used in the following circumstances:

- Your feet are tied together and/or provide your only means of defense
- You *must* hit two persons simultaneously
- You use fixtures or opponents for support
- Attack is overpowering, risk is justified
- Your skills are flawless, risk is negligible

9. Twin Front Kick

Jump straight up as high as possible, pulling both knees close to the chest. Lean your upper body toward the target as you snap both legs forward, with feet together. Quickly retract both legs to prepare for the landing. If you lose balance or cannot prepare the landing, execute a Back Fall.

10. Twin Roundhouse Kick

Jump straight up with your legs tightly tucked, and your knees and feet together. Snap both legs forward with the feet close together, striking with the Instep Foot or Ball Foot. If you lose balance or cannot prepare the landing, execute a Side Fall.

11. Twin Side Kick

Jump straight up or use a running start for forward velocity. Thrust both legs forward with the feet close together, striking simultaneously with the Bottom Heels or soles of both feet. Keep your upper body over your hips. If you lose balance or cannot prepare the landing, execute a Side Fall.

12. Twin Back Kick

Jump straight up and thrust both legs backward with feet close together, striking with Bottom Heels. If you lose balance or cannot prepare the landing, execute a Front Fall.

13. Twin Front Split Kick

This is executed similar to a Twin Front Kick, except you will hit two opponents simultaneously at your left and right sides, with your feet spread apart. If you lose balance or cannot prepare the landing, execute a Back Fall. For most people, this is the easiest twin kick to learn and apply.

14. Twin Side Split Kick

This is basically a Side Kick and a Front Kick combined. Targets include both heads, trunks, or knees. Jump straight up, turning your body 90° in the air as you bring the knees high, with your body leaning forward (left knee toward chest, right knee pointing forward). Extend both legs at the peak of the jump. Do not lean back, or a balanced landing will be difficult. This kick is difficult.

9. Twin Front Kick

10. Twin Roundhouse Kick

11. Twin Side Kick

12. Twin Back Kick

13. Twin Front Split Kick (view left to right)

14. Twin Side Split Kick (view left to right)

Practical Use of Your Surroundings

Normally, *Jump Twin Kicks* require a high degree of skill, since you must kick with both feet while airborne and return safely to the ground. This is quite difficult. However, these same kicks can also be executed by using your environment to assist the kick, making them quite practical and much easier to execute safely. This might involve use of permanent fixtures, furniture, architectural details, or the attackers themselves (when fighting multiple opponents). Practical use of your surroundings might typically involve the following situations:

- You jump off higher surfaces to gain height (e.g., table, chair, car hood, fence).
- You grasp an overhead fixture for support (e.g., pipes, chains, conduit, door header, hanging lamp, industrial equipment).
- You support your body with both hands on chairs, tables, handrails, or other fixtures.
- You vault over an obstacle, using your hands for support.
- You are restrained and hanging freely from an overhead support by your arms.
- You are held from behind (supported by one opponent while you kick the second).
- You support yourself by holding on to, or pressing down against, one or more attackers as you strike another.
- You vault over an injured attacker (bent-over or kneeling), using your hands for support, to strike another attacker.
- You step on and jump off a reclining attacker to gain height to strike another.
- You cushion your landing by falling onto a soft surface (e.g., dirt, trash, bedding, water).

Many martial artists dismiss unusual or highly specialized techniques such as twin kicks, claiming they are impractical or useless. The following examples are not meant to be recommended defenses for specific situations, but merely illustrate how *any technique* (in this case twin kicks) can become highly practical or even necessary, given an appropriate situation. Think creatively and keep an open mind.

Twin Front Kick (bear-hug from behind, held aloft)

Twin Back Kick (hands on chair or table)

Twin Side Kick (hands on chair or table)

Front Split Kick (restrained in a chair, hands behind back)

Side Split Kick (forced back into chair)

Twin Front Kick and Choke (forced back onto table top)

Front Twin Kick (restrained in a chair, feet tied together)

Front Split Kick (hanging from doorway molding)

Side Split Kick (hanging with hands tied to an overhead fixture)

Twin Side Kick (vaulting over injured attacker)

Twin Back Kick (choking front attacker for support)

Front Split Kick (hanging, hands restrained overhead)

Overhead Split Kick (forced back onto table top)

Scissor Kick-Throw (holding left-attacker for support)

Head strikes and body strikes, commonly called butts, are hitting techniques that use specific surfaces of the head, shoulder, chest, or hip for delivering blows to a range of vulnerable targets. These techniques are not as frequently used as hand and foot strikes, but are very practical in certain circumstances, particularly when your hands or feet are restrained or otherwise occupied. Because your head, shoulder, and chest are highly susceptible to damage, these blows must be applied properly with a judicious use of force directed

HEAD + BODY STRIKES

to appropriate targets. Otherwise you may injure yourself as well as your opponent. Exercise caution when executing head butts: repeated blows to the head, regardless of force, produce cumulative and permanent brain damage, and may contribute to permanent neurological disorders. This chapter outlines 10 head and body strikes used in the martial arts. The following pages provide an overview of basic principles and a description of each strike, outlining their biomechanical qualities, appropriate uses, and relationships to each other.

HEAD AND BODY STRIKES

Virtually any part of the human body can be an effective striking weapon, with proper training and in an appropriate situation. Although the majority of strikes used in most martial arts are executed using the arms and legs, certain circumstances may necessitate the use of other body surfaces, such as the hips, shoulders, chest, and head.

Because many of these surfaces are very susceptible to damage, proper technique and target selection is essential, particularly when executing head strikes. Most head and body strikes are normally used in conjunction with other techniques, since they are not normally considered to be finishing or devastating techniques on their own. Normally used at close range or when grappling, they can be used to escape a hold, create space when you are being held or crowded, or set up other techniques by distracting an opponent.

Head and body strikes might normally be used in the following situations:

• You are fighting at close range
• Your limbs are restrained or damaged
• Your arms or legs are being used
• You are being choked
• You are grappling or fighting on the ground
• You wish to upset an opponent's balance
• You are assisting a throw or takedown
• It is the best response in a given situation

1. Forehead Butt

Before executing any head butt, bend your tongue up against against the roof of your mouth and close the jaw. This will strengthen the neck and channel Ki to your forehead. Always hit with the thickest part of your skull (frontal area below hairline). A Forehead Butt is used at close range to strike the nose, eyebrows, temple, cheek, spine, sternum, or ribs. Short straight thrusting blows are used for maximum power. Glancing blows directed to cranial nerves or soft, cut-prone skin are also highly effective and pose less risk to you. Try to target pressure points, since less force is required for the blow to be effective.

Use of any Head Butt implies a certain element of risk to yourself, which must be justified by circumstances. Although your blow may stun the opponent, you may also give yourself a concussion or skull fracture, or open a cut. Repeated blows to the head, regardless of force, produce cumulative and permanent brain damage.

2. Side Head Butt

This can be either a thrusting or a glancing strike. It is often used when an opponent's head is alongside yours or slightly higher. The hitting area is the thick part of your skull *above* the temple. Targets include the face, nose, ears, and underside of the chin (hit up).

Forehead Hitting Surface

Side Head Hitting Surface

Back Head Hitting Surface

Chin Hitting Surface (teeth clenched)

1.1 Forehead Butt (thrusting strike to bridge of nose at M-HN-3 and M-HN-4)

1.2 Forehead Butt (glancing strike to eyebrow at M-HN-6 and forehead at GB-14)

3. Back Head Butt

This strike is normally used if you are being held from behind, particularly when your arms or feet are restrained. It is also used to butt upward, hitting the underside of the chin. This can cause an opponent to crack a tooth, or to bite their own tongue, lip, or inner mouth if the jaw is unclenched. Since it is not a knockout strike, it is used to set up other techniques by creating a distraction or space to maneuver. The nose, face, or underside of the chin are common targets. Use light strikes only.

4. Head Thrust

This thrusting strike is directed to the spine or abdomen (soft targets only). The head is aligned with your upper body as you drive forward, pushing off with your back leg. It is commonly used when your hands are restrained, and is similar to certain tackling methods used in American football. Take care not to compress your cervical vertebrae.

5. Chin Press

This is a very short, light thrusting strike directed to sensitive nerves or acupoints. A Chin Press is typically used to release a choke by attacking nerves on the choker's lower arm, or to release a bear-hug from the front by attacking sensitive points on the sternum (e.g., CO-17). It is essential to clench your teeth to prevent your lower jaw from moving, since motion can transmit stress to your temporomandibular joints (back of jaw). Powerful strikes are considered inappropriate, since you will likely damage your jaw.

6. Biting

For most animals, the teeth constitute a major weapon. In humans they do not, due to social conditioning as well as millions of years of evolution that have made our jaws structurally inadequate for this type of fighting. Nonetheless, biting can be a very useful, and sometimes lifesaving, technique. When your arms and legs are restrained, or you are held in a submission hold or pin, or other forms of attack are ineffective, biting an opponent may constitute your only option.

If you are being smothered by a hand held over your mouth and nose, open your mouth and bite into the fingers or palm. If you are being choked by an attacker's arms or legs, bite into the limb. If you are being pinned to the ground by a body-press against your head, bite into the chest or abdomen. If you are being sexually assaulted, bite the attacker's lips, tongue, nose, cheek, ear, or anything else forced into or near your mouth.

Be aware that bites which break the surface of the skin allow exchange of diseases transmitted by bodily fluids. Since biting attacks cannot be practiced, training can only involve mental preparation or recognition of opportunities present during practice fighting.

2. Side Head Butt (to nose)

3.1 Back Head Butt (to escape bear-hug hold)

3.2 Back Head Butt (upward to underside of chin)

4. Head Thrust (to abdomen or solar plexus)

5. Chin Press (pressing into LI-7 against a choke)

6. Biting (to escape choke hold)

7. Shoulder Butt

This is a thrusting strike in which you hit with the meaty part of your shoulder around the upper arm. Exercise caution since the shoulder is easily damaged. Shoulder butts are typically used to unbalance an opponent, create space to set up other techniques, break the elbow during arm bars, or assist certain takedowns (e.g., a single-leg takedown with a Shoulder Butt to the inner knee).

8. Chest Butt

This strike is executed by thrusting your chest forward as you pull your shoulders backward. To avoid having the wind knocked out of you, *Kihap* and retain your breath as you strike. Chest Butts are typically used to unbalance or knock the wind out of an opponent by striking the chest, usually when your hands are restrained. Chest Butts are also used to create space to set up other techniques, break the elbow during cross-chest arm bars,

or drop on top of a fallen opponent, often when pinning. Body drops to a fallen attacker can be very dangerous, since the full weight of your body crashes into the opponent.

If an opponent is lying on their back, drop onto their chest or abdomen (loss of breath, broken ribs, organ trauma), or head (broken nose, concussion, neck trauma). If an opponent is lying on their side, targets are usually the head or shoulder (shoulder separation, torn rotator cuff). If an opponent is lying on their stomach, drop onto their back or head.

9. Side Hip Butt

This is a thrusting strike directed sideways, using the side of your hip. The hitting surface is the area indicated by the protruding femur bone (greater trochanter). Side Hip Butts are commonly used to upset an opponent's balance, knock them to the ground, assist execution of certain hip or leg throws, or

counter a hip or shoulder throw by thrusting your hip into the attacker's hip. Side Hip Butts can also be used to drop sideways on top of a fallen opponent, often as part of a throwing technique. Typical standing targets include the opponent's hips, abdomen, buttocks, groin, upper leg, and knee. When executing hip throws (see *Throwing* chapter), your initial hip-plant to the opponent's upper leg or groin can be changed to a strike by simply generating greater horizontal force as you step inward and pivot.

10. Back Hip Butt

This is a thrusting strike directed backward, using the buttocks. It is typically used to create space or set up other techniques, when you are held from behind. This butt is also used to assist hip throws as described under the *Side Hip Butt*, or to fall or drop on top of a fallen opponent, sometimes as part of a throwing technique.

7.1 Shoulder Butt (unbalancing opponent)

7.2 Shoulder Butt (striking and breaking elbow as wrist is pulled)

7.3 Shoulder Butt (striking inner knee to assist a takedown)

7.4 Shoulder Butt (striking upward to underside of chin)

8.1 Chest Butt (breaking the elbow; note assisting forearm strike)

8.2 Chest Butt (unbalancing strike to attacker's chest; hands restrained behind back)

8.3 Chest Butt (dropping onto head during ground fighting)

9.1 Side Hip and Shoulder Butt (dropping onto groin and chest after throwing)

9.2 Side Hip Butt (striking groin to assist a hip throw)

9.3 Side Hip Butt (striking lumbar spine to assist choke and unbalance attacker)

10.1 Back Hip Butt (striking backward to groin and abdomen, to escape a bear-hug)

10.2 Back Hip Butt (dropping onto spine of thrown opponent; note ankle hold)

Real combat is rarely decided on the basis of a single technique. The ability to execute combinations of techniques and make transitions from one technique to another is crucial, as is the ability to recognize these opportunities during the flow of combat, which is constantly changing. For every technique, there is a counter; and for every counter, another counter. The more skillful your opponents are, the more easily they will move to negate your attack or defense. Strikes can fail for any number of reasons, such as your technique

COMBINATIONS

is too slow, your opponent blocks or avoids the blow, or the dynamics of a situation change as you launch a blow and the strike is no longer feasible. For this reason, it is important to develop skills that allow you to intuitively apply combinations and transitions as needed. Since this is a book about striking, combinations in this chapter will involve strikes linked to strikes. Naturally, strikes can also be linked to holds, throws, or any other technique that is appropriate—an approach covered in the author's 1136-page book, Hapkido.

The 160-plus strikes previously outlined can be linked into sequential combinations in almost limitless ways. The number of possible combinations might fill 10 books alone—this would not even begin to include combinations linked to holds and throws. Typical strike combinations are listed on the following pages, and are organized into three groups: *Arm Strike Combinations*, *Kick Combinations*, and *Mixed Combinations*.

All examples apply to confrontations with a single opponent, unless otherwise noted, and can be used for attack or defense. Note that left (L) and right (R) designations can be switched. You should always practice combinations from both sides (switching your lead), since injuries or the dynamics of a fight may force you to respond from your weak side. Practice from relaxed and fighting stances. When learning new combinations, practice slowly, gradually increasing speed. Never execute techniques faster than your level of skill permits, otherwise you ingrain bad habits that are difficult to unlearn and correct later.

ARM STRIKE COMBINATIONS

The combinations listed opposite can also be practiced by substituting other hand strikes, while maintaining the same basic delivery. For example, a "L Jab Punch–R Hook Punch" combination might become:

L Spear Hand (4 fingers) to throat
R Middle Finger Fist (hook) to ribs (LV-13)

L Spear Hand (2 fingers spread) to eyes
R Thumb Fist (hook) to ribs (SP-21)

L Tiger Mouth to throat
R Index Finger Fist (hook) to ribs

L Palm Heel to solar plexus
R Inside Back Fist to temple

L Straight Back Hand to face
R Thumb Hand (hook) to ribs

Since many other combinations are possible, experimentation is encouraged.

Fore Fist Leads

L Jab Punch
R Straight Punch

L Jab Punch
R Overhead Punch

L Jab Punch
L Uppercut Punch

R Straight Punch to head (rear hand)
L Hook Punch to ribs (lead hand)

L Uppercut Punch
R Uppercut Punch

L Uppercut Punch
L Hook Punch
R Hook Punch

R Uppercut Punch
L Turning Hammer Fist

L Hook Punch to midsection
L Hook Punch to head

L Jab Punch to face
R Straight Punch to face
L Hook Punch to ribs
R Uppercut Punch to groin or midsection

L Jab Punch
R Straight Punch to solar plexus
L Hook Punch to head
R Straight Punch to face

L Jab Punch to face
L Hook Punch to ribs (while ducking)
R Uppercut Punch to chin

L Jab Punch
R Hook Punch to midsection (ducking)
L Hook to head
R Uppercut to groin or midsection

L Jab Punch
R Hook Punch to midsection
R Hook Punch to head
L Uppercut Punch to groin or midsection

L Jab Punch
R Inside Knife Hand to ribs

R Jab Punch (lead hand)
L Straight Punch (rear hand)
R Knuckle Fist uppercut to top of throat (lead)

R Jab Punch to face, or Knuckle Fist to throat
L Vertical Punch to solar plexus
R Descending Back Fist to face

R Jab Punch to face (lead hand)
L Straight Punch to solar plexus (rear hand)
R Back Fist to temple (lead hand)

L Straight Punch to face (from relaxed stance)
R Straight Punch to solar plexus
L Straight Punch to groin

R Straight Punch to groin (relaxed stance)
L Straight Punch to face
R Straight Punch to solar plexus

Typical Arm Strike Combination (L Jab Punch, R straight Palm Heel Strike, L Inside Elbow Strike)

Back Fist Leads

L Back Fist to temple
R Inside Knife Hand to neck or ribs
L Spear Hand to throat (ST-9, 10 or CO-22)

L Back Fist to temple
R Turning Back Fist or Hammer Fist
or R Turning Knife Hand or Elbow Strike

R Snap Back Fist to temple (from side stance)
L Vertical Punch to solar plexus
R Snap Back Fist to groin
(or reverse order of strikes)

R Back Fist to temple
R Outside Eagle Hand to ribs (SP-21)
L Palm Heel to solar plexus

R Back Fist to temple
R Back Elbow Strike (while stepping in)
R Open Hand to groin (quick slap)
R Descending Back Fist to face

R Back Fist to temple
L Inside Elbow Strike to midsection
R Inside Elbow Strike to head

R Back Fist to temple
L Inside Elbow Strike to head
R Rising Elbow Strike to solar plexus and chin
R Outside Hammer Fist to ribs

L Back Fist to nerves on lead hand or arm
R Straight Punch to head
L Knuckle Hand to groin or solar plexus

Open Hand Leads

L straight Palm Heel or Open Hand to nose
R Ox Jaw to solar plexus
L Hook Palm Heel to side of jaw

R Spear Hand to eyes (lead hand)
L Vertical Punch to solar plexus
R Inside Palm Heel to temple, or side of nose

R Outside Knife Hand to neck (or slash eyes)
L Inside Knife Hand to ribs
R Descending Knife Hand to neck

L Outside Knife Hand to head (jamming)
R Uppercut Punch (Middle Finger Fist)
R Hook Punch to neck at LI-18 (Middle Finger Fist)

L Circular Ridge Hand (or Palm Heel) to temple
R Turning Knife Hand to neck

L Spear Hand to groin area (LV-12, SP-12)
R Palm Heel Hand upward to side of jaw (ST-5)

L Tiger Mouth or Pincer Hand to throat (ST-10)
R Knuckle Hand uppercut to ribs (LV-14)
R Chicken Hand hook to temple (LI-18)

L Palm Heel to solar plexus (rear hand)
R Inside Elbow Strike to jaw (lead hand)

R Ox Jaw Hand to solar plexus
R Eagle Hand to groin (while turning)
R Relaxed Back Hand to nose (descending)
L Descending Elbow to collarbone or spine

R Straight Back Hand to face
L Vertical Punch to solar plexus
R Inside Knife Hand to neck
or R Descending Snap Back Fist to nose bridge

Opponent standing close behind, to your left
L Five Fingertip or Claw Hand to groin
R Back Punch to face, step back + pivot 180°
R Outside Elbow Strike to kidneys or spine

Forearm Leads
(usually from a relaxed stance or close range)

L Outside Forearm Strike to head
R Inside Elbow to ribs
L Rising Elbow Strike to groin or chin

L Outer Forearm Strike to head (jamming)
R Rising Bent Wrist Strike to groin
R Turning Outside Elbow to skull or kidney

R Outside Forearm Strike to head
Collapse arm, R Inside Elbow Strike to head
L Rising Elbow Strike to groin

Opponent in side stance
L Outside Forearm Strike to face (lead arm)
R Hook Punch to solar plexus

R thrusting Outer Forearm Strike to nose
L Five-Fingertip Hand to groin
or R Rising Elbow Strike to solar plexus

R Inner Forearm Strike to temple or neck
L thrusting Outer Forearm Strike to nose

Standing close in front
L Outer Forearm Strike to nose (thrusting)
R Hook Forearm to back of skull (BL-10), choke

Bent Wrist Leads
(from a relaxed walking stance)

R Rising Bent Wrist to chin
R Inside Knife Hand to neck
L Straight Palm Heel to nose (R hand pulls head)

R Rising Bent Wrist to groin
R Descending Back Fist to face
L Knuckle Fist hook to ribs (SP-21)

R Rising Bent Wrist to chin
L Rising Bent Wrist to groin
R Eagle Hand to eye (forearm vertical)

Elbow Combinations (close fighting)

R Rising Elbow Strike to chin
R Back Elbow Strike to solar plexus

L Rising Elbow Strike to chin
R Descending Elbow Strike to collarbone

L Inside Elbow Strike to head
R Descending Elbow Strike to collarbone

R Inside Elbow Strike to midsection
L Inside Elbow Strike to midsection
R Inside Elbow Strike to head

R Inside Elbow Strike to head
L Inside Elbow Strike to midsection
R Rising Elbow Strike to chin or groin

R Assisted Side Elbow Strike to face
R Back Elbow Strike to solar plexus

L Inside Elbow Strike to head
R Turning Outside Elbow to kidney or spine

KICK COMBINATIONS

The basic kicks previously outlined can be combined in limitless ways. Common combination kicks are listed on the following pages, and pertain to a single opponent unless otherwise noted. Always practice combinations from both leads, since injury or the dynamics of a confrontation may force you to respond from either side.

Today, many martial artists believe that using continuous combinations of kicks can leave you vulnerable to throws, particularly against skilled grapplers. Consequently, kicking skills tend to be less emphasized today than in past decades. Nevertheless, continuous, fluid combinations of kicks might become important if your arms are restrained or damaged during the course of a fight, or if you need to create space against multiple attackers.

Basic Tactics

When creating combination kicks, the first kick is often designed to set up the second kick, and can be anything from a feint to a powerful strike. Even when feinting, you must cause your opponent to take the first kick seriously, otherwise the second kick may be detected and countered. The second or third strikes are usually reserved for your strongest techniques. Another tactic is to strike a low target first (e.g., groin or knees), in order to lower the head for the second kick. This *head lowering* can be the result of a damaging blow or merely a reflex action on the part of your opponent. Otherwise, single high kicks are easily countered and may leave you vulnerable to a variety of throws and strikes.

When practicing kick combinations, a fundamental objective in most martial arts is to make *two or more sequential kicks into one fluid motion*. For this reason, the second kick is often a jump kick. For example: in a normal combination kick (e.g., left Front Kick, right Roundhouse Kick), your second kick is executed after your first kicking leg is returned to the ground. The time between kicks can be shortened by executing the second kick *before* planting your foot.

Front Kick Leads

L Front Ball Kick to midsection
R Front Heel Kick to chin

L Front Kick to belly or groin
R Roundhouse Kick to head

L Front Toe Kick to groin
R Side Kick to knee (or midsection)

L Front Blade Kick to groin
R Inside Axe Kick to head

L Front Kick to midsection (opponent retreats)
R Drop Spin Kick to ankles

L Front Instep Kick to groin
R Rising Knee Strike to face (pull head down)

Shin Kick Leads

R Shin Kick to lower leg (opponent retreats)
L Side Kick to knee or midsection
R Turning Back Kick to midsection or head

R Shin Kick to lower leg
R Roundhouse Kick to outer knee or head

R Shin Kick to lower leg
R Side Kick to knee
L Turning Hook Kick to head

R Shin Kick to lower leg
L Inside Hook Kick to outer knee
R Rising Knee Strike to abdomen (pull opponent)

Roundhouse Kick Leads

L Roundhouse Kick to outer knee
R Roundhouse Kick to head
L Uppercut Back Kick to midsection

R Roundhouse Kick to outer knee
R Roundhouse Kick to head

R Roundhouse Kick to outer knee
R Side Kick to midsection
L Turning Back Kick or Hook Kick
or L Spin Kick takedown to both legs

R Roundhouse Kick to outer knee
L Roundhouse Kick to head
R Drop Spin Kick to ankles

R Roundhouse Kick to groin (using ball foot)
Bent-over opponent: L Inside Axe Kick to spine
Upright opponent: L Shin Kick to lower leg

R Roundhouse Kick to outer knee
(attacker back steps changing stance)
L Turning Back Kick (to open side)
R Roundhouse Kick to head or groin
or R Hook Kick to head or knees

R Roundhouse Kick to outer knee
(attacker back slides, same stance)
L Turning Back Kick (to closed side)
L Back Kick (to open side)

R Roundhouse Kick to outer knee (attacker backs
away, same stance), cross-step forward
R Back Kick (to open side) with front leg

Typical Kick Combination (R Side Kick, L Turning Uppercut Back Kick, R Rising Knee Strike)

L Roundhouse Kick to outer knee
R Spin Kick to head
L Inside Axe Kick
or L Roundhouse Kick to ribs

L Roundhouse Kick to groin
R Spin Kick to head
R Front Kick to midsection

L Roundhouse Kick to outer knee
R Hook Spin Kick to same knee

L Roundhouse Kick to outer knee
R Hook Kick to head (no spin)

R Roundhouse Kick to outer knee
L Rising Knee Strike to head
L Stamp Kick to top of foot

R Roundhouse Kick to inner knee (don't plant)
R Side Thrust Kick to opposite inner knee

R Roundhouse Kick to groin (ball foot)
L Turning Uppercut Back Kick

L Reverse Roundhouse Kick
R Spin Kick

L Reverse Roundhouse to head (opponent at side)
R Roundhouse Kick to groin
R Side Kick to knee

Side Kick Leads

R Side Snap Kick to shin
L Turning Uppercut Back Kick
R Inside Axe Kick to collarbone

R Side Snap Kick to knee
L Turning Uppercut Back Kick
R Inside Hook Kick to knee

R Side Snap Kick to shin
R Side Thrust Kick to knee
R Roundhouse Kick to knee (using instep or shin)

Cross-step forward
R Side Kick to midsection (front leg)
L Front Kick

Crescent Kick Leads
(usually for blocking or head strikes)

L Inside Crescent Kick
R Turning Uppercut Back Kick
L Roundhouse Kick to outer knee

L Inside Crescent Kick
R Spin Kick

R Inside Crescent Kick (don't plant foot)
R Side Kick to midsection or knee
L Turning Back Kick to midsection or head

R Outside Crescent Kick
L Inside Crescent Kick
R Turning Outside Crescent Kick

Kick Leads Used at Close Range
(usually avoiding a punch or moving in close)

R Inside Hook Kick to outer thigh (GB-31)
R Stamp kick to top of foot
R or L Rising Knee Strike to face (pull head down)

R Side Knee Strike to front of thigh
R Stamp Kick to top of foot

R Stamp Kick to foot diagonally across
R Rising Heel Kick to groin
R Stamp Kick to other foot

R Low Spin Kick to knee (stepping forward)
L Roundhouse Kick to head
If too close: L Inside Crescent Kick to head

Cross-step forward
L Hook Kick to knee
R Turning Back Kick to head
or R Hook Spin Kick to head

R Inside Hook Kick to knee (with rear leg)
Set leg down in rear position
L Rising Heel Kick to groin
If bent over: R Inside Heel Hook to spine
If head is raised: R Back Kick to midsection

Against Charging Opponent
(usually while stepping or jumping backward)

R Side Kick to midsection (lead leg)
L Turning Back Kick to midsection
R Hook Kick to head (turn right)

L foot steps back from L lead, R Back Kick
L Turning Uppercut Back Kick to head
R Roundhouse Kick to outer knee

L Back Kick to midsection (front leg)
R Spin Kick to head or knee

R Rising Back Kick to shin (blade foot)
L Uppercut Back Kick to head

R Hook Kick to head (fade-away)
L Turning Back Kick to midsection

R Spin Kick to head (no step, rear leg kick)
R Drop Spin Kick to ankles

Against Side or Push Kick

R Rising Front Kick to underside of kick leg
L Turning Back Kick

L Rising Front Kick to underside of kick leg
R Spin Kick or Drop Spin Kick

R Rising Blade Kick to kicking leg (use side step)
L Turning Uppercut Back Kick to midsection

R Rising Blade Kick to kicking leg (use back step)
L Hook Spin Kick to head or knee

L Rising Blade Kick to kicking leg
R Drop Spin Kick to ankles

R Rising Blade Kick to kicking leg
Skip step, R Side Kick to inner knee of support leg

R Axe Kick to kicking leg
R Roundhouse Kick to groin (ball foot)

R Blocking Blade Kick to kicking leg
L Roundhouse Kick to back of knee
(kick same leg as they plant it)
R Roundhouse Kick to head (as they bend)

MIXED COMBINATIONS

After you have mastered arm strikes and kicks separately, they can be combined into mixed combinations using any of the 160-plus strikes outlined in earlier chapters. The specific dynamics of a situation, and your own imagination and skill, are the only limitations. Building your own personal vocabulary of combinations is suggested, since this will strengthen your ability to spontaneously improvise at length, leading to confidence and proficiency in self-defense situations. Use combinations that are suited to your own body characteristics, physical limitations, and philosophical ideals regarding "acceptable use of force." The examples listed opposite are common applications. Countless other possibilities exist.

When developing new strike combinations, use the following suggestions as a guideline. They are not meant to be rigid rules, but a summary of the fundamental principles that define many practical combination strikes. In the end, any technique that works is a good technique, regardless of rules.

- Alternate between different types of strikes.
- Vary striking distance and body position to make countering difficult.
- Keep initial kicks low unless a clear opening is present.
- Strike targets at different heights.
- Maintain constant movement and a varied rhythm to your attack. Be unpredictable.
- Avoid complex changes in hand or leg formations which slow execution speed.
- When closing in on an opponent, use kicks to close the distance, followed by hand strikes as you move closer.
- When moving away from an opponent, use arm strikes to create space, followed by kicks as distance increases.
- Strikes should follow one another in a natural flowing progression. The motions of the preceding strike will suggest and generate movements that naturally lead into subsequent strikes.

Hand Strike Leads

L Jab Punch
R Front Kick (rear leg)

L Jab Punch
R Turning Back Kick

L Jab Punch
R Straight Punch
R Front Kick (rear leg)

L Hook Punch to ribs
R Turning Uppercut Back Kick

L Hook Punch to ribs (lead hand)
R Spin Kick (while stepping back)

R Uppercut Punch
L Uppercut Punch
R Turning Back Kick

Foot Strike Leads

Cross-step forward, R Side Kick (lead leg)
L Straight Punch

L Front Kick (front leg)
R Straight Punch

L Front Kick (front leg)
R Uppercut Punch

R Reverse Roundhouse Kick to leg
R Back Fist to head
L Uppercut Punch to midsection

R Reverse Roundhouse Kick to back of knee
L Overhead Punch to head
R Roundhouse to groin (ball foot)

L Roundhouse Kick to knee or groin (rear leg)
Opponent is bent over
R Descending Hammer Fist to cervical spine
R Front Knee Strike to sciatic nerve in buttock

L Roundhouse Kick to knee (rear leg)
R Uppercut Punch to midsection
L thrusting Outer Forearm to face

L Roundhouse Kick to knee or groin (rear leg)
R Turning Knife Hand to neck
L Uppercut Punch

L Roundhouse Kick to outer knee
R Turning Hammer Fist to ribs

R Roundhouse Kick to outer knee
R Back Fist to head
L Vertical Punch to solar plexus
R Palm Heel upward to side of jaw (ST-5)

L Side Kick
R Overhead Punch
L Inside Knife Hand to ribs

L Side Kick
R Hook Punch to head
L Knuckle Fist Uppercut to top of throat

R Turning Back Kick to midsection
L Straight Punch to Head
R Hook Palm Heel to side of nose

Typical Mixed Combination (R Descending Hammer Fist, R Inside Crescent Kick, R Side Kick)

R Turning Back Kick to midsection
L Circular Ridgehand to neck
R Spear Hand to groin
L Shin Kick

R Inside Hook Kick to knee or thigh
R Circular Ridgehand to neck (ST-9, ST-10)
L Straight Punch to face
R Uppercut Punch to groin

R Inside Crescent Kick
L Turning Knife Hand to neck

Cross-step forward
R Hook Kick
R Back Fist
L Uppercut or Straight Punch

R Axe Kick
L Uppercut Punch

L Back Fist to face
R Inside Crescent Kick to face
R Back Fist to ribs

Umbrella Strike
Hit three opponents simultaneously.
One opponent is standing in front,
the other two are standing to either side.
(technique is shown in the photos below)
A) Bring both hands to your hips, chamber R leg
B) Thrust both your fists and R leg outward,
like opening an umbrella:
R Straight Punch to front opponent
L Straight Punch to left opponent
R Side Kick to R opponent

Umbrella Strike: Simultaneous Twin Knuckle Hand Strikes and Side Kick

Strikes are an important form of attack and defense found in a great many martial arts. Strikes are also quite likely the most common form of attack encountered during self-defense and combat, situations that typically involve marginally trained opponents who lack sufficient skills to execute effective holds and throws. Consequently, it is not only important to master the strikes themselves, but also common methods of avoiding or blocking these same blows. Avoiding and blocking techniques are also very important for setting

AVOIDING + BLOCKING

up counterattacks, since they optimize body position while helping prevent injury. It is often said that without an adequate defense there can be no offense. This chapter will present an overview of basic principles and common techniques used in Hapkido, which are also found in other martial arts. Recognize that these techniques are not only used to initiate counterstrikes, but to also enter a range of joint locks, chokes, and throws, as shown in the author's companion books The Art of Holding and The Art of Throwing.

Overview

Avoiding and blocking techniques are used to prevent being hit, pushed, or grabbed by either armed or unarmed attackers. These techniques usually involve blocking a strike by using your arms or legs, although blows are also avoided by body movement or neutralized by absorbing the blow's force.

Blocking techniques are usually thought of as *defensive*, although a well-timed, powerful block to an appropriate target (joints, small bones, nerves, pressure points) can easily damage your opponent's limbs, leaving them unwilling or unable to continue the fight. In this sense, a block can also be a form of attack, similar to a strike. While blocks can be singular techniques, they are usually combined with strikes, holds, and throws to initiate counterattacks. Later chapters will cover blocking-and-striking. The author's other books cover entries to holds or throws.

Generally speaking, to neutralize a blow you must commit one of the following actions, either singularly or in combination:

- *Avoid* the strike by removing yourself from its path.

- *Block* the blow by acting upon it with sufficient force to alter its path or stop its motion.

- *Absorb* the force of the strike to diffuse its power (when you cannot avoid being hit).

Avoiding

The safest and most desirable method for neutralizing a strike is to avoid it entirely. This may involve ducking, a quick movement of the head, turning or leaning the upper body, or stepping in any direction to establish distance (usually to the side or backwards). Avoiding is usually an integral part of blocking, although *avoiding and striking* (without blocking) is often used to execute very fast counterstrikes. This is quicker than blocking and countering, but also riskier. However, against a highly skilled opponent, it may be required to neutralize the attack.

Blocking

A block interrupts the intended path of a strike by deflecting it away from its target, or stopping its motion entirely. The degree of force required depends upon the type of block and its intended result. Blocks may be executed by using the hands, arms, legs, or torso against all forms of strikes. Most blocking techniques are also accompanied by body movements designed to protect yourself should the block fail. In this sense, *avoiding* is almost always an integral part of blocking.

Absorbing

When you cannot avoid a strike, you must attempt to diminish its effect by absorbing its force. This is usually accomplished by withdrawing the target in sync with the incoming strike, thereby diminishing the force at impact. *Absorbing* can also involve placing another, less damageable, part of your body in the path of the strike. For example, raising your arms to cover up and absorb punches directed to your head. This will probably be painful, but is infinitely more desirable than absorbing blows with your skull. Absorbing principles are also an important part of many blocking and countering techniques that involve grabbing and redirecting an attacker's limb into a hold or throw. In these situations *absorbing* is essential, since it provides the extra time needed to seize control of the attacker's limb.

Types of Blocks

This chapter documents 50 common blocks. These blocks utilize both linear and circular motions, and can involve actions such as thrusting, snapping, glancing, parrying, pressing, trapping, grabbing, pushing, and absorbing. Some blocks are used extensively in many different self-defense techniques, while others are only appropriate in very specific situations. Preferences for certain blocking techniques will also vary by martial art. If one were to organize blocks by their function (which is one of several possible methods of classification), they would generally fall into the following categories:

- Deflecting Blocks
- Grabbing Blocks
- Opposing Blocks
- Striking Blocks
- Shielding Blocks

Methods of Neutralizing a Strike

Avoiding

Blocking

Absorbing

Deflecting Blocks

Deflecting blocks redirect the path of a strike by using the force of the block to alter the strike's trajectory. This may involve light pressing or parrying movements designed to deflect the blow using minimal force (called soft blocks), or powerful focused blocks designed to deflect the blow while also damaging the attacker's limb (called hard blocks). Both types of blocks have advantages and disadvantages. Soft blocks require less power and expenditure of energy, possess greater speed, are very useful against overpowering opponents, and minimize damage to yourself. Hard blocks are a better deterrent, since they also cause pain or injury. However, you are also more likely to damage your own blocking surfaces unless they are well conditioned. If your limbs become injured during a fight, hard blocks cannot be used.

Grabbing Blocks

Grabbing blocks are light *deflecting blocks* in which you keep your hands close to the attacker's arm or leg throughout the block, immediately grabbing the limb as soon as it is safely redirected past you. Avoid excessive force when blocking; otherwise, the attacker's arm will be knocked away, out of your reach. Grabbing blocks are usually linked to strikes, holds, or throws.

Opposing Blocks

Opposing blocks stop the motion of a strike by acting upon it with greater opposing force. Since opposing blocks are essentially strikes employed for blocking purposes, the entire body is used to add force to the block. Hip and shoulder rotation, leg thrust, arm snap, and weight transfer—all the fundamentals of striking—are also used when blocking. Naturally this poses an element of risk, since you may also damage your own limbs. Consequently, forceful opposing blocks are not advised against overpowering opponents who possess greater bone mass. Opposing blocks are most effective when a strike is blocked early in its delivery, before it has time to develop greater force; or when combined with blending motions that reduce impact.

Striking Blocks

These are not really blocks per se, since the blow is neither deflected nor stopped. Rather, they are strikes targeted to the attacking arm or leg. First, one avoids the strike by moving out of its path. As the strike is fully extended (just before retracting), the defender strikes a vulnerable nerve, pressure point, muscle, or joint on the attacker's extended limb, using any appropriate strike. Some of the more common striking blocks (e.g., Back Fist Strike) were covered in earlier chapters.

Shielding Blocks

These blocks absorb the force of a blow by placing the arms or legs in the path of the strike, thereby protecting a more vulnerable target, such as the head, neck, solar plexus, ribs, or groin. Commonly called *covering up,* this type of block is usually only used when you cannot avoid being hit, or you are engaging a much smaller opponent who's blows are light and ineffective. Against a very fast striker delivering blows too fast to block, shielding may be your best and only option.

Types of Blocks

Deflecting Block (soft style)

Deflecting Block (hard style)

Grabbing Block

Opposing Block

Striking Block

Shielding Block

AVOIDING TECHNIQUES

The following evasive techniques are used to avoid blows without moving your body out of striking range. They can be executed without stepping or blocking, leaving both hands or feet free to counter. They can also be linked to blocks and steps, which makes them safer and provides greater assurance that you will not be hit. However, in certain circumstances stepping and blocking is neither possible (strikes are too fast to block or step away from), nor desirable (you wish to remain close to the opponent to execute counterattacks).

Avoiding techniques are often preceded by feints, which draw specific attacks from your opponent. Knowing which attack is coming allows you to plan and time your response. For example, you feint *forward motion* using head movement. Your opponent believes you are moving in and responds with a hook punch to the head. You duck forward to avoid, and counter with an uppercut to the groin.

Avoiding skills require good timing, reflexes, anticipation, and lots of practice. In Western boxing, kick boxing, and just about any other form of full-contact fighting, avoiding skills are considered to be vitally important, and are an integral part of any superior fighter's repertoire. If your hands are restrained behind your back or maneuvering space is limited (you can't step away), avoiding skills might even become essential. Practice the following seven techniques from relaxed and fighting stances, against a variety of strikes. After you are proficient, link them to striking, holding, and throwing counters, as well as to footwork.

Avoiding Techniques

Technique	Movement
1 Slipping	left-right
2 Ducking	up-down
3 Leaning Back	backward
4 Body Rolling	away from blow
5 Body Turning	trunk rotation
6 Body Swaying	up-down, left-right
7 Stepping Away	any direction

1. Slipping

Slipping is used to avoid straight strikes to the head, by shifting your head to either side of the blow. Execute by quickly turning the shoulders, as you lean to the side and slightly forward, turning the head and shoulders as a unit (1.1, 1.2). Turn and lean in the same direction, so that the punch slips over the shoulder turning toward the attacker (*slipping right* passes the punch over left shoulder; *slipping left* passes the punch over right shoulder).

1.1 Slipping right (against straight strikes)

1.3 Slipping inside from open stances

1.5 Slipping inside from closed stances

Do not move your head separately unless you must compensate for inadequate movement. Shifting the weight to the front or rear leg during the turn is important, and largely determined by stance relationships (open or closed) and hand use (rear or lead). Precise timing, quick reflexes and anticipation are very important if the technique is to be successful. Slip at the last possible instant, moving only enough to barely avoid the blow. If you slip too early, the attacker will adjust or

1.2 Slipping left (against straight strikes)

1.4 Slipping outside from open stances (safer)

1.6 Slipping outside from closed stances (safer)

catch you with a different blow. You may slip to either side of a punch, although slipping to the *outside of a lead punch* is considered safest and opens your opponent to a variety of counterattacks that are difficult to defend against. When slipping inside and counterpunching, you can hit harder, but are more vulnerable to attack. Counterpunching from a slip is faster and more powerful than blocking and punching, since shoulder rotation used during the slip also develops punching power.

2. Ducking

Ducking is mostly used to avoid circular or hooking strikes directed to your head. This includes Hook or Roundhouse Punches, Outside Knife Hand Strikes, Roundhouse Kicks, Hook Kicks, and Spin Kicks. To execute, drop the head and upper body forward by bending at the waist or knees. As the blow passes, rise up to either side in a circular motion (2.1). This motion makes targeting your head more difficult, compared to rising straight up. Bend at the waist and knees when you wish to counter from a standing position (2.2). Bend at the knees when you wish to counter with a drop kick or move to the ground (2.3). Otherwise, deeply bending the legs momentarily limits mobility, slows footwork, and reduces counterpunching power.

3. Leaning Back

Leaning Back is used to avoid straight, circular, or hooking strikes directed to your neck or head. Execute by snapping the head and upper body backward, and shifting weight to the rear leg. As the strike misses, quickly return forward (3.1). The move is characterized by a back and forward rocking motion— quick, continuous, and fluid. The body must be loose and relaxed. Try to keep the shoulders level. A typical counterattack might involve leaning back to avoid a rear hand punch, then snapping forward as the attacker's fist retracts, delivering a lead punch to the ribs (3.2). Counters can also be executed during the backward motion without returning forward. For example, lean back to avoid a Side Kick, instantly countering with a lead Rising Blade Kick to the underside of the leg (3.3).

2.1 Ducking (used against circular and hooking strikes)

2.2 Ducking and countering a Hook Punch

2.3 Ducking a kick (bending low to set up a takedown)

3.1 Leaning Back (used against any form of strike; snap back and quickly return forward)

3.2 Leaning Back, countering with Uppercut Punch

3.3 Leaning Back, countering with Rising Blade Kick

4. Body Rolling

When you cannot avoid being hit, Body Rolling reduces the force of a blow by moving your body in unison with the strike. This is the origin of the common expression: "rolling with the punches." The direction you roll depends on where the strike is coming from, and is always away from the blow. Generally, circular strikes require lateral movement (4.1, 4.2), straight strikes require backward movement (4.3), and overhead or descending strikes require a downward circular movement to either side (4.4). Body rolling can be linked to footwork if time permits, and is often used with shielding blocks for greater protection.

5. Body Turning

Body Turning is used to avoid a straight strike directed to your head or trunk when standing in a relaxed or frontal fighting stance, facing your opponent. To execute, turn the shoulders and hips as you shift your body laterally, pivoting on the balls of feet without stepping (5.1). It can also be preceded by a short side step, when time permits. Body Turning is often linked to blocks or holds, and is excellent for counterpunching—particularly with your lead hand during the initial shoulder rotation (5.2).

6. Body Swaying

Body Swaying (also called "bob and weave") is a term that refers to two separate methods of evasive movement which are often performed together. These movements involve swaying the upper body in a disjointed, non-rhythmic fashion, in order to evade and confuse your opponent, disguise your attack, and make accurate targeting of your head and trunk difficult. Body Swaying is also used to move under an opponent's attack and deliver strikes from close range. It is very useful against taller opponents, or when attempting to get close to execute a throw or takedown against strikers. Basically it resembles *Slipping* and *Ducking* linked into a single continuous, deceptive, unpredictable, evasive movement. Body Swaying is usually an important element in any modern fighter's repertoire, although the manner in which it is applied can vary widely by martial art.

4.1 *Body Roll lateral (against Hook Punch)*

4.2 *Body Roll lateral (against low Roundhouse Kick)*

4.3 *Body Roll backward (against Side Kick)*

4.4 *Body Roll down and lateral (descending strike)*

5.1 *Body Turn (no steps; quick return to guard)*

5.2 *Body Turn against straight punch (countering with Hook Punch to head)*

6.1 *Body Swaying (bobbing inside, then weaving outside)*

6.2 *Body Swaying (Bobbing outside, then Weaving inside)*

6.3 *Body Swaying while counterpunching (Bobbing and Weaving)*

6.4 *Slipping outside with right Hook, then weaving to the inside with left Uppercut (countering a lead straight punch)*

Bobbing

Bobbing is based on *Ducking* and involves a rising and falling movement of the head, which is sometimes coordinated with shoulder rotation. The motion can be either straight up and down, or resemble a "V," with the head and upper body moving as a unit. Bend the knees to generate the movement, maintaining your normal guard as you rise and fall. Bobbing is mostly used to avoid circular or hooking strikes to the head, while setting up counterattacks. When using a "V" movement, rotate the shoulders as described under *Slipping*.

Weaving

Weaving is based on *Slipping* and involves a dipping circular movement of the head and upper body, to the left or right. The motion resembles a "U," with the head and upper body moving as a unit. To execute, bend both legs to lower the head. As the head moves sideways and upward, rotate the rear shoulder forward. Weaving can place your body on the opposite side of an opponent's centerline, setting up a counterattack. Weaving is also used to move the body in, out, and around a straight lead punch to the head (6.3). Weaving usually follows a Slip and is often used to keep counterattacking with both hands. For example, counter with a right punch as you slip outside, followed by a left-right combination as you weave inside (6.4). Generally speaking, Weaving is usually used in conjunction with Bobbing.

7. Stepping Away

You can also avoid a blow by stepping away from your opponent. This usually involves stepping sideways, backward, or 45° forward. Basic steps were covered previously under *Movement*. For speed and safety, keep steps quick and short. It is only necessary to move far enough to avoid the attack or set up a counterattack—unless you are attempting to run away. Steps can be used with any of the six avoiding techniques previously discussed. Stepping makes *avoiding* generally safer, but will reduce the speed of your counterattacks, since stepping takes valuable time.

SOFT BLOCKS (PARRIES)

Soft deflecting blocks (commonly called parries) are light, fast, pressing movements of the hands or forearms, designed to deflect a blow using minimal force. Parries constitute the core of any modern fighter's defensive technique. Of all the blocks covered in this section, parries are probably the most important, since they are easily learned, highly practical, and can be used against a wide variety of attacks and styles. They are also excellent for generating counterattacks.

Parrying Fundamentals

When executing parries, timing and speed is far more important than power. Do not reach out toward the strike, but allow the blow to come to you, deflecting it at the last moment. Reaching outward allows your opponent to alter the delivery and creates openings for other strike combinations. Do not use the same type of parry repeatedly, since your opponent will detect this and capitalize on it. Instead mix different parries, varying rhythm and cadence to generate confusion and disrupt an opponent's attack plan. Parries can be used with any of the *avoiding movements* covered previously. Against large, aggressive, or powerful attackers (taller, longer reach), step laterally or backward as you block.

Ideally you will parry a blow using the *palm, knife-edge,* or *back of the hand,* although the *forearm* is also used, particularly against strikes to the trunk. Keep the elbow fairly stationary, close to your ribs for protection. Parry outward from your midline, returning to guard after each parry. When blows come in very quickly, it's not always possible to be selective with blocking surfaces. Remember, the important thing is to *deflect,* without compromising your defense. Specific mechanics will vary based on circumstances and the stances you operate from.

In Hapkido, most parries consist of three types of movement: *short* (simple motion, 3 to 12"), *semicircular* (hand traces a 90 to 180° arc), and *circular* (hand traces a 360° arc, returning to the original position). Typical examples are shown on the following pages.

1–6 Short Parries

Short Parries are defined by a brief, quick, precise movement in any direction, to deflect a blow away from your body. Move the hand only enough to deflect the blow, quickly returning to guard. The *return to guard* may also be used to parry another blow. If you move your hand too far, you will be vulnerable to feints or disengaging strikes (strikes that pause in mid-delivery, then continue), since the hand will be too far away to execute the next parry in time. Short Parries are most effective against straight strikes, pushes, or attempts to grab. Circular or hooking strikes usually require other forms of blocks.

1. *Inside Parry (lead hand)*

(rear hand)

2. *Outside Parry (lead hand))*

(rear hand)

3. Descending Parry (lead hand)   *(rear hand)*

4. Rising Parry (lead hand using palm-up option)   *(rear hand using back-hand option)*

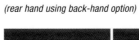

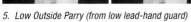

5. Low Outside Parry (from low lead-hand guard)   *(from low rear-hand guard)*

6. Low Inside Parry (from low lead-hand guard)   *(from low rear-hand guard)*

7–8 Semicircular Parries

In Semicircular Parries, the hand traces a 90–180° arc in front of your body, from low to high, or high to low. The elbow acts as a fulcrum and should remain fairly stationary and near the side of the body, where it can be used to protect your ribs and midsection. Semicircular Parries are normally used to:

• Engage a low strike from a high guard
• Engage a high strike from a low guard
• Redirect a high strike to a low position
• Redirect a middle strike to a low position
• Provide defensive cover
• Disguise your tactics
• Set up attacks or counters

The parrying movement occurs in one of two directions: from high to low, or low to high. In both motions, the parrying hand redirects the blow outward to the side, away from your body. When executed from an opponent's outside it will open inside targets. When executed from an opponent's inside, it will open outside targets. When directed downward from high to low, a Semicircular Parry can be used to engage a blow at any height, during any point in the parry's 180° motion. When directed upward it is usually only used to engage a higher strike, near the end of the parrying motion. This might occur immediately after parrying a low blow (your hand is low and must be brought back upward). Do not redirect low strikes upward to high positions, since you will probably guide the punch into your head.

Defensive Cover
Certain types of attacks are inherently difficult to defend against. When fighting a highly skilled opponent who constantly feints and/or is very fast with punches (faster than your reactions), any parry or block can be difficult to properly time. In these troubling situations, Semicircular Parries can be used to provide a constant defensive motion, before your opponent strikes. One or both hands alternate in a non-rhythmic, asymmetrical, disjointed manner, executing parries in both directions (up-down, down-up). Although you may not be able to time the blow, it is still likely that the parry will engage the strike, since it is already moving. During execution, vary the range of motion and the hand combinations (singular or both); above all, do not be predictable or your opponent will time the strike to land ahead of, or behind, your parry. Your parrying movements are not only for blocking, but should also generate confusion and disrupt your opponent's tactics. As a result, continuous parries are often useful in staging offensive attacks. This constant and varied movement will also keep you loose and relaxed, quickening your reaction time to changes in attack. Both lead and rear hand use is illustrated in the accompanying photos.

7. Downward Semicircular Parry (lead hand)   (rear hand)

8. Upward Semicircular Parry (lead hand)   (rear hand)

Semicircular Parry: Engaging a low strike from a high position

Semicircular Parry: Engaging a high strike from a low position (after blocking)

Semicircular Parry: Redirecting a high strike to a low position (never low to high)

Semicircular Parry: Redirecting a middle or low strike to a low position

Defensive Cover

Sequence showing continuous short and semicircular parries used for defensive cover (constant movement, varied rhythm, single hand movements, combined hand movements)

Parrying Multiple Strikes

Sequence lasting about 1 second: R Outside Parry to L Jab, R Inside Parry to L Jab, R Rising Parry to R Straight, L Semicircular Parry to Front Kick (defender sliding backwards).

9–10 Circular Parries

In circular parries, the hand traces a 360° arc in front of your body, in a clockwise or counterclockwise direction. The elbow and wrist act as a fulcrum, as previously described under *Semicircular Parries*. When compared to Short Parries and Semicircular Parries, Circular Parries are slower, but protect a larger area and are more difficult to deceive with feints. They are often used to enter wrist holds, or gain the inside position when countering with strikes, holds, or throws. Circular Parries are normally used to:

• Redirect a strike out to the side
• Redirect and lead into a wrist hold
• Redirect and lead into a hold or throw (e.g., arm bar, choke, passing throw)
• Unbalance an attacker by redirecting force
• Provide defensive cover
• Disguise your tactics, distract
• Set up attacks or counters

Execution

Meet the attacker's wrist with your hand or forearm, just before the blow lands. Wrap the wrist as you redirect the arm in a circular path, returning your hand to its original position. This movement can also be used to execute two blocks—one in the beginning and a second block as your hand returns to its starting position. This is useful if you have responded to a feint, or if an attacker retracts and strikes again with the same hand.

The *size of the circle* may vary depending upon the desired result. Large circles protect broader areas and are useful for unbalancing a clumsy opponent. However, they take longer to execute, allowing the attacker greater time to withdraw the hand and strike before your motion is completed and your hand returns to a safe position. Small circles are faster, safer, and more efficient when blocking, but do not unbalance or redirect the body as effectively.

The size of the circle is varied by elbow placement and elbow extension. The wrist, elbow, and shoulder can all be used as pivot points to varying degrees, which also influences the size of the circle. Experiment to see how various methods of execution affect speed and coverage.

Transitions to Holds and Throws

Circular parries are often used to deflect a strike and make a transition to holds or throws—in a single fluid movement. Common transitions include wrist holds, arm bars, chokes, leg takedowns, hip throws, and head lock throws. These techniques are covered in the author's other books (p 207).

Defensive Cover

Similar to Semicircular Parries, Circular Parries can also be used to disrupt an opponent who feints or is very fast, by providing a constant defensive motion.

9. Outside Circular Parry (lead hand)   (rear hand)

10. Inside Circular Parry (lead hand)   (rear hand: works best when lead hand is low)

Outside Circular Parry used to block two strikes

Inside Circular Parry used for defensive cover (defender reacts to feint, but blocks blow on return motion).

Circular Parry with transition to wrist grab (twisting and pulling arm to set up strikes, holds, or throws)

Circular Parry with transition to wrist grab, followed by Outer Forearm Strike to neck to set up throw

11–12 Grab Parries

A Grab Parry is basically a *Short Parry* which changes into a wrist grab. It is used to pull an attacker off-balance, enter holds or throws, or set up counterstrikes by briefly restraining the hand or pulling the attacker into your strike. It is executed with either hand from the opponent's inside or outside, against straight strikes or shoves from either hand. Speed is essential in order to grab the punch before it is retracted. Grab Parries can be executed using *avoiding movements,* or by stepping in any direction (when time permits). When combined with a blending step, they can also be used against circular strikes. There are two basic types of Grab Parries: *Outside Grab Parry* (using an outward motion) and *Inside Grab Parry* (using an inward motion). Four basic variations are shown at right.

11. Outside Grab Parry

Parry with the knife-edge or back of the hand using minimal force, so that attacker's arm remains near your parrying hand. Immediately turn your hand outward, wrapping it over and around the lower arm or wrist (the wrist is ideal, but not always possible). Use the turning movement of your hand to carry it toward the wrist. As you near the wrist, form a *ring* with your thumb and fingers. The ring will stop the hand when it reaches the wider girth of attacker's fist. This secures your grip, allowing you to pull or redirect the arm. You may also grab loose clothing or a sleeve.

12. Inside Grab Parry

This is similar to the previous technique, except it begins with an *Inside Short Parry* which changes into a wrist grab. It is used for the same purposes as the *Outside Grab Parry* (see previous parry). When compared to the outside version, the *Inside Grab Parry* sets up for different types of counterattacks. Parry with the palm, then grip the wrist or sleeve with an overhand grip. The thumb either wraps over or under the wrist, based on the countertechnique you will be applying. *Wrapping under* provides a more secure hold when you will be pulling the arm, and permits transitions to a wider range of wrist holds.

11. Outside Grab Parry (from opponent's outside)

Outside Grab Parry (from opponent's inside)

12. Inside Grab Parry (from opponent's outside)

Inside Grab Parry (from opponent's inside)

13. Combined Grab Parry (with lead hand parry crossing over rear hand grab)

Combined Grab Parry (with lead hand parry crossing under rear hand grab)

14. Two-Hand Grab Parry (moving to opponent's outside)

Two-Hand Grab Parry (moving to opponent's inside; note simultaneous elbow strike)

13. Combined Grab Parry

In rapid sequence, execute a *Short Parry* with one hand, followed by a *Grab Parry* using the opposite hand. The first parry deflects while the second parry grabs—unless the first parry fails, in which case the second parry deflects and grabs. Both parries should be executed in close sequence, appearing to be a single move at first glance. Because one parry follows the other, you have a greater margin for error, are less likely to be affected by feints or disengaging blows, and have a greater chance of grabbing fast punches when compared to single parries. It is mostly used against straight strikes or pushes.

The *Combination Grab Parry* can be executed with innumerable variations based on which hand parries first (lead or rear), which hand crosses over or under, and whether the parry is executed from the attacker's outside or inside. These factors are influenced by stance relationships (open-closed), strike height, and the hand which is striking (lead or rear).

14. Two-Hand Grab Parry

This parry uses both hands to deflect a blow, while grabbing the attacker's arm or leg. It is used to pull an attacker off-balance, enter holds or throws, or set up counterstrikes by pulling the attacker into your blow (e.g., knee strike to the torso). To apply, simultaneously execute an *Inside Grab Parry* with your lead hand, and an *Outside Grab Parry* with your rear hand, grabbing the attacker's arm at the wrist and upper arm with both hands. This parry is normally used against straight thrusting strikes, from relaxed or fighting stances; or, when combined with a blending step, it can also be used against circular strikes. A *Two-Hand Grab Parry* is usually executed by stepping to the opponent's outside (safer), where it can be linked to a variety of counterstrikes, holds, and throws. When stepping inside (riskier), it is often linked to strikes that assist throwing techniques (e.g., inward elbow strike to chin, then Inner Reap Throw). This parry can also be executed as two separate hand movements, similar to the *Combination Grab Parry* previously discussed.

151

HARD BLOCKS

When compared to soft blocks (see previous pages), hard blocks use many of the same basic motions, but *generate* or *absorb* greater force for a variety of purposes. Hard blocks can be used to counter strikes, pushes, holds, and attempts to grab or choke. They can involve different types of blocking actions, such as deflecting, opposing, striking, and shielding—all of which were defined at the beginning of this chapter.

Blocking surfaces include the forearm, hand, elbow, upper arm, leg, and foot. Most of these surfaces are formed using the same *attack points* used for striking. In hard blocks, force is generated by using twisting, snapping, thrusting, or turning movements of the body or limbs, which are designed to focus force at the moment of impact—similar to a strike. The degree of force used is variable and depends upon the type of block, size of opponent, force of attack, direction of attack, and strength of your own blocking surfaces. Determining where a soft block ends and a hard block begins is difficult and of no practical consequence. Like parries, hard blocks can be integrated with various forms of avoiding movement and footwork.

Many of the blocks in this section are illustrated using both long-traditional and short-modern deliveries. Generally, long deliveries are only used to teach basics, or when the arm *must move* from one distant location to another. For example: defending from relaxed stances, alternating between low and high blows with the same arm, or alternating between multiple attackers.

Forearm Blocks

Forearm blocks use the hard edge of the ulna or radius bone to execute blocks against all forms of attack—high, low, straight, circular, rising, descending, arm strikes, leg strikes, etc. The blocking surface is the hard area extending from the wrist upward about 3 to 4 inches. When executing forearm blocks, you must use your blocking surfaces accurately, since there are many sensitive nerves and

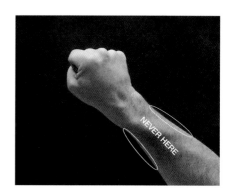

Forearm blocking surfaces: edge of ulna or radius bone

Hand formation during forearm blocks: vary to suit subsequent techniques; may be open, closed, loose fist etc.

15. Rising Block

Rising Block using short delivery

16. Descending Block

Descending Block using short delivery

17. Outside Low Block

Outside Low Block using short delivery

pressure points also present in the immediate vicinity; inaccurate blocking can easily damage your own arm. Generally, the ulna can withstand greater force than the radius.

When executing forearm blocks a variety of open hand or closed hand formations can be used, depending upon tactics and preference. *Closed hand* formations protect the fingers from being accidentally jammed, or attacked with finger holds; and permit quick transitions to punches. *Open hand* formations promote greater fluidity (sometimes) and allow quick transitions to grabbing holds, throws, or open hand strikes. In almost all forearm blocks, twisting and rotating the arm during delivery is crucial to develop focused force at impact. Shoulder and hip rotation and rear-leg thrust can also be used to generate power *when there is time*. Whenever possible, direct the block to the part of the attacker's arm or leg, where nerves or pressure points are present.

15. Rising Block

This block is used to deflect high straight strikes, circular strikes, or descending strikes directed to the head. Block upward, from underneath the blow, using a rising motion as you twist the ulna-side of your forearm into the attacker's arm or leg. Your forearm should finish at an angle, with the arm slightly above and in front of the head. Against circular or hook strikes, the delivery is slightly outward.

16. Descending Block

This block is used to deflect straight or rising strikes directed to the lower abdomen or groin. Block straight down, from above the blow, using a descending motion as you twist the ulna-side of the forearm into an attacker's arm or leg. Your forearm finishes parallel to the ground, with the palm of your fist facing you. It resembles a *Rising Block* in reverse.

17. Outside Low Block

This is similar to the previous *Descending Block*, except the attack is deflected down and to the side, away from your body. It is one of the most basic and important methods for deflecting low strikes or kicks.

18. Inside Low Block

This block is used to deflect low straight strikes to the lower abdomen or groin. The twisting forearm follows an inward path across your body and deflects the strike to the side, using the ulna-side of forearm. Finish with the palm facing up. It is usually executed with the lead hand, since rear hand blocks are obstructed by your own body—unless you are simultaneously back stepping, so that the rear hand becomes the lead hand.

Outside Low Blocks (see previous page) and *Inside Low Blocks* are often executed sequentially (in any order) when defending against multiple low strikes or feints. This makes for very quick, efficient blocking, since the finishing position of one block leads to the beginning of the other. Their combined movements should be short, rapid, and focused, similar to the manner in which *Short Parries* are linked. Always articulate the twist of the forearm to generate speed and power. Practice these and other combinations until they are fluid and instinctive.

19. Inside Block

This block is used to deflect straight or circular strikes directed at the head or midsection. The forearm follows an *inward* path across your body and deflects the blow to the side, as you twist the ulna-side of your forearm into the attacker's arm or leg. The forearm should finish vertical or at a slightly forward angle, bent about 90° at the elbow. For greater power (time permitting), rotate the shoulders and hips in unison with the delivery, pull the opposite hand toward your chest or hip, and tense the musculature around your armpit as you make contact. When speed is required, abbreviate or eliminate these supporting movements.

An Inside Block can be executed while stationary or moving in any direction, with either hand. It is a fundamental block found in many martial arts systems. Whether you use a long or short delivery, the twisting of the forearm is essential for transmitting a focused shock on impact.

18. Inside Low Block

Inside Low Block using short delivery

19. Inside Block

Inside Block using short delivery (open hand option)

20. Outside Block (palm facing rear)

Outside Block using short delivery

21. Reverse Outside Block (palm facing forward)

Reverse Outside Block using short delivery

20. Outside Block

Like the previous *Inside Block,* this block is also used to deflect straight or circular strikes directed at the head or midsection— except it travels in the opposite direction and uses the opposite side of the forearm for blocking. The forearm follows an *outward* path across your body and deflects the blow to the side, as you twist the radius-side of your forearm into the attacker's arm or leg. Finish with the palm facing toward you. During the delivery the elbow acts as a pivot and is fairly stationary, as you drive the hand upward and forward. The forearm should finish at a forward angle, and is bent about 90° at the elbow.

For greater power, rotate the shoulders and hips, as you pull the non-blocking hand in the opposing direction toward the chest or hip. The hips may rotate in either direction (with or opposing the block), similar to the Back Fist strike variations described in the *Arm Strikes* chapter. Whether you use a long or short delivery, the twisting of the forearm is essential for transmitting a focused shock on impact. When initially defending from a relaxed stance (hands at side), this is one of the quickest hard blocks you can execute.

21. Reverse Outside Block

This block uses the ulna-side of the forearm to deflect straight or circular strikes to the head or trunk. When compared to the previous Outside Block, the *Reverse Outside Block* is often considered a better choice against hook punches or circular strikes. The forearm follows an *outward* path across your body and deflects the blow to the side, as you twist the ulna-side of the forearm into the attacker's arm or leg. Finish with the palm facing forward and the elbow aligned with your body; the elbow is bent about 90°.

When defending from fighting stances, this block is a very quick and simple method of deflecting. Against fast punches or feints, it is often used in alternating combinations with *Inside Blocks,* since the finishing position of one is the start of the other—similar to the manner in which *Short Parries* are linked.

22. Pressing Forearm Block

This block uses an *opposing* action to trap the attacker's arm, as they begin their delivery. The block is usually used against an Uppercut Punch, but is also effective against an opponent who punches from the hip. It is most practical at close range or when you are charging inward. Direct the block to an attacker's inner elbow or forearm.

23. Scissor Block

This is an *Outside Block* and an *Outside Low Block* executed in unison. It is used to bend or break the elbow during a single-arm push or grab; or to deflect two simultaneous attacks to a high and low target, such as the head and groin. It is mostly used against a Twin C-Punch, attempts to grab, or simultaneous attacks from two attackers. As you block, your hands travel in opposing circular paths (elbow fulcrum). A full delivery is shown, but is often shortened in actual use.

24. High X Block

This is basically two *Rising Blocks* executed with the wrists crossed. It is used to block straight strikes or descending strikes to the head. Block upward from under the blow, as you cross your wrists and twist the ulna-side of your forearms into an attacker's limb. Your hands may be either open or closed, similar to other forearm blocks. In addition to blocking punches, the High X Block is also used to trap and grab an opponent's punching arm. The Low X Block, a variation used to block straight or rising kicks, is shown later in this chapter under *Blocks Against Kicks.*

22. Pressing Forearm Block (to inner elbow at biceps tendon; against uppercut punch)

23. Scissor Block

Scissor Block deflecting a Twin C-Punch   Scissor Block used to bend or break the elbow during a one-hand push

High X Block against a Straight Punch to face

24. High X Block

25. *Outside Knife Hand Block (to wrist at LI-5)*

26. *Inside Knife Hand Block (to tendons above wrist at PC-6)*

27. *Side Ox Jaw Block*

28. *Descending Ox Jaw Block (to tendons above wrist at PC-6, or forearm at LU-6; against uppercut punch)*

HARD BLOCKS USING THE HANDS

The following blocks are executed using specific attack points on your hand. These same surfaces are also used for striking. Deliveries are usually based on the same motions used in strikes or forearm blocks. When compared to forearm blocks, accuracy is more important, since the blocking surface is smaller, and the hand is easily damaged by incorrect technique. Hand blocks are usually directed to nerves or pressure points.

25. Outside Knife Hand Block

This block uses the Knife Hand to deflect strikes directed to the head or trunk. The hand follows an outward path and deflects the strike to the side using the edge of the hand—as if you were chopping the hand off at the wrist. Finish with your palm facing forward, and the elbow aligned with your body, bent about 90°. This block is executed similar to a *Reverse Outside Block* (see #21).

26. Inside Knife Hand Block

The Knife Hand follows an inward path across your body and deflects the strike to the side. Finish with the palm facing up. It is used to block strikes directed to the chest or head. The delivery is similar to an *Inside Block.*

27–28 Ox Jaw Blocks

This is basically an Ox Jaw Strike modified for blocking. It is used against straight or circular strikes to the head, trunk or groin. The block is usually directed downward or horizontally into the attacking arm or leg. To execute, snap the wrist forward as you pull the hand back, blocking with the edge of the hand.

27. Side Ox Jaw Block

This block is directed sideways into the attacking limb, and is used against straight or circular strikes to the upper chest or head.

28. Descending Ox Jaw Block

This block is directed downward into the attacking arm or leg, against straight strikes to the abdomen or groin, or rising uppercuts. From a fighting stance, quickly drop either hand as you snap your wrist.

SHIELDING BLOCKS

Shielding blocks absorb the force of a blow by placing your arms or legs in the path of the strike, thereby protecting a more vulnerable target, such as the head, neck, solar plexus, ribs, or groin. Commonly called *covering up,* this type of block is usually used when you cannot avoid being hit, wish to appear helpless, or you are fighting a much smaller opponent whose blows are light and ineffective. Against a very fast striker delivering blows too fast to block or avoid, shielding may be your only defensive option. When skillfully applied, shielding blocks can also be an excellent base for launching counterattacks.

29. Head Block

This shielding block uses the arm to protect the side of the head and neck. Raise your arm with the elbow fully closed and the fist tightly clenched (to reduce damage to the hand). Against very powerful blows, press your arm against your head to prevent the force of the strike from slamming your fist into your own head. Against an opponent in front, this block would be used to defend against circular strikes such as the Hook Punch, Roundhouse Kick, Hook Kick, and Spin Kick. In these instances, try to step toward the opponent's body, placing your head inside the blow—this reduces the impact on your arm and head.

30. Face Block

This block uses both arms to protect the front of the face, neck, chest, and solar plexus—absorbing the force of the strike. Raise your arms with the forearms together, the fists clenched, and the elbows covering the chest.

31. Body Block

This shielding block uses the arm to protect the body and head. It is similar to a *Head Block,* except the elbow is placed lower to protect more of your body. Raise your arms with the forearms covering your ribs, and the hands protecting your face. Lower your head and tuck your chin in against your shoulder or chest. Allow your body to turn and sway with the strike, to reduce its impact. This is often called "rolling with the punches."

29. Head Block

Head Block against circular punches to side of head

30. Face Block

Face Block against straight punches to the face

31. Body Block

Body Block against repeated kicks to the ribs and head

32. Groin Block

Groin Block against attacker crashing in with their knee

33. Catching Block (as strike nears full extension)

Catching Block (before strike is extended)

34. Jamming Block (charging inward to smother the attack)

Blocks from Ground Positions (with simultaneous counterstrikes)

Parry to straight punch, Palm Heel Strike to CO-15.

Outside Block to Hook Punch, Tiger Mouth Strike to throat

Grab Parry to Straight Punch, Palm Heel Strike to elbow

Elbow Wrap Block to Hook Punch, Elbow Strike to head

32. Groin Block

This shielding block is used to protect the groin and genitalia from low punches or kicks, by pivoting the hip or thigh into the line of attack. If you are being overwhelmed, it can be combined with a *Body Block*.

33. Catching Block

This shielding block is used to smother a punch early in its delivery, or catch a strike as it nears full extension, by placing the open palm in the path of the blow. It is usually used against very fast strikes (e.g., lead jabs), which are difficult to block using other techniques. If your timing is good, catching blocks can also be used to briefly redirect the punch as you counter with the other hand. Against a slower or weaker striker, it is sometimes possible to grab the fist.

34. Jamming Block

Jamming is a technique used to smother an opponent's attack before it can be launched. As soon as you sense the attack (or during a pause in the attacker's offense), charge inward with your arms and legs protecting vital targets, as you crash into his body. Use your arms, legs, and body to press his limbs into his own body, as you apply close range strikes, holds, and throws. This technique is not recommended against a much larger, stronger, or heavier opponent, since you will probably be knocked off-balance.

BLOCKS FROM GROUND POSITIONS

Most of the blocks used while standing can also be executed from various ground positions, such as kneeling, seated, reclining, mounting, or being mounted. The photos at left show typical scenarios with blocks linked to simultaneous counterstrikes. Since body movement is restricted and the opponent is very close, risk is compounded. Therefore, short, quick, simple blocks are suggested. The following types are generally most useful.

• Short Parries (to deflect)
• Grabbing Parries (to trap the arms)
• Forearm Blocks (inside, outside, rising)
• Shielding Blocks (when other blocks fail)

BLOCKS AGAINST KICKS

Many of the blocks previously covered can be used very effectively against kicks. Some of these include the Low Block, Outside Block, Inside Block, and most forms of parries. Additionally, there are also a number of specialty blocks designed to be used against kicks. These are shown on the following pages. These blocks often set up transitions to specific strikes, holds, and throws.

Generally, the weight, mass, and power generated by the kicker's leg is substantially greater than that of your blocking arms or hands. Consequently, blocks against kicks usually involve blending and absorbing movements to reduce the impact of the kick on your blocking surfaces. Hard blocks (using reduced force) should be directed to sensitive nerves or pressure points to be safe and effective. If you attempt to block powerfully using bone against bone, it is likely you will damage your own arm. Regardless of the block you use, remember to protect your fingers, toes, or other damageable parts from direct contact with the full force of a kick.

35. Outside Scoop Block

Use the palm of either hand to deflect and grab straight thrusting kicks directed to low and middle targets. The hand follows a downward circular path, catching the ankle with your open hand as you pull and lift, while deflecting outward. By lifting the foot, you make it difficult for the attacker to retract the leg or maintain balance—very useful during transitions to strikes, holds, or throws. When time permits, step sideways or backward while blocking, for greater safety. Against fast snapping kicks, Scoop Blocks become very difficult to time. Most of the previous discussion also applies to the *Hook Blocks* and *Wrap Blocks* discussed subsequently.

36. Inside Scoop Block

This is similar to the *Outside Scoop Block,* except the hand sweeps inward, in the opposite direction. The block can be executed with either your lead or rear hand. When possible, step sideways or backward while blocking.

35. Outside Scoop Block

36. Inside Scoop Block

37. Outside Hook Block

38. Inside Hook Block

39. *Outside Wrap Block*

40. *Inside Wrap Block*

41. *Middle-Low Block*

42. *Two-Hand Wrap Block*

37. Outside Hook Block

This block is very similar to an *Outside Scoop Block,* except you will block and lift with the forearm, along the radius bone (thumb-side). The block can be applied *softly* by blending with the kick's motion, or *forcefully* by striking the leg muscles. The delivery resembles a *Hook Punch* directed upward.

38. Inside Hook Block

This is similar to the *Outside Hook Block,* except the forearm sweeps inward, similar to an *Inside Scoop Block.*

39. Outside Wrap Block

This block is used to trap and hold the leg as you execute strikes and throws. Begin with an *Outside Hook Block, Outside Scoop Block,* or *Low Block* and continue wrapping your arm around the knee, lower leg, or ankle. Clamp your arm closed like a vice, trapping the leg.

40. Inside Wrap Block

This is similar to the *Outside Wrap Block,* except your arm sweeps inward, in the opposite direction.

41. Middle-Low Block

Simultaneously execute a *Low Block* with your lead hand, and an *Inside Middle Block* with your rear hand. Against circular kicks, such as the Roundhouse or Spin Kick, it can be used to provide a forceful block, shield a broad area, or set up a transition to a *Two-Hand Wrap Block* (see next block). Since the Middle-Low Block protects both low and high targets, it is often used against fast, proficient kickers, who are capable of beating or deceiving your blocks. It is also safer for individuals with slow reactions. Use blending footwork to reduce the impact on your arms.

42. Two-Hand Wrap Block

This block is applied in one of two ways:
1) execute an *Inside Middle Block,* then an *Outside Wrap Block;* or 2) execute a *Middle-Low Block* and wrap the leg with your lower arm. This block is used to trap the leg, setting up a variety of takedowns and throws. It is used in many Hapkido kick defenses.

43–44 Back Fist Blocks

These blocks are basically Back Fist Strikes to nerves on the leg. They are used against Front or Side Kicks to discourage further attack, or reduce mobility by damaging the leg.

43. Descending Back Fist Block

This is directed to points on the ankle and instep (e.g., LV-3 or GB-41); or can be used to break the toes, which are quite fragile when shoeless. It is not necessary to use much force, since the foot is accelerating into your fist. Execute with the lead hand while stepping backward. Use a quick, short circular delivery, quickly returning to guard. Keep your fist clenched to avoid damaging the hand.

44. Raking Back Fist Strike

Target nerves on the shin or calf. Step sideways as you rake the leg, striking multiple points in a single motion. For Side Kicks, hit into the front or rear edge of the fibula. For Front Kicks, hit into the sides of the tibia.

45. Descending Elbow Block

This block is basically a short elbow strike. Simply move your elbow into the kick's path, allowing the the foot to crash into the point of your elbow. A slight downward motion can be added for greater impact. Because this block requires little motion, it is very deceptive and may appear to be unintentional. It is most effective against Front and Roundhouse Kicks (strike the instep). Against Side and Back Kicks, use a pronounced downward strike.

46. Descending Palm Heel Block

Snap your Palm Heel Hand straight down into the leg, deflecting a low straight or rising kick. Against rising kicks, do not block forcefully or you may damage your hand. Block lightly as the leg is fully extended, while stepping back.

47. Low X Block

Block with both Palm Heel Hands, or forearms (ulna side). Block down to either side of the shin, with your arms crossed at the wrists. You may also block to the top of the ankle or foot. Front Kicks are the primary application. This block is also used to trap and grab the ankle.

43. Descending Back Fist Block (while stepping back)   44. Raking Back Fist Block (while stepping sideways)

45. Descending Elbow Block (against Front Kick)

46. Descending Palm Heel Block

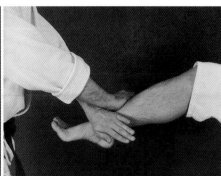

47. Low X Block (against Front Kick)

48. Inside Leg Block

Inside Leg Block against Roundhouse Kick

49. Outside Leg Block

Outside Leg Block against Roundhouse Kick

50. Rear Leg Block

Rear Leg Block against Roundhouse Kick

Inside Leg Block against Rising Knee Strike

Outside Leg Block against Roundhouse Knee Strike

48–50 Leg Blocks

In Leg Blocks, the lower leg or thigh is raised to either *shield* or *deflect* kicks directed to the abdomen, groin, or legs. Avoid hard contact with sensitive nerves located along the shin. Leg Blocks are one of the simplest and most effective means for protecting lower targets against a variety of kicks, as shown in the examples at left. Because the leg is raised, it is also ideally positioned to execute an immediate kicking counterattack. After blocking (or kicking), *immediately* return your foot to the ground. Remember, from the moment you raise your leg until you put the foot down, your mobility is limited and your balance is vulnerable (one-point balance). Grapplers will often feint a kick to bring your leg up, then crash inward to execute a throw.

Leg blocks can be executed using the lead or rear leg, with the knee placed at a variety of locations and heights—depending upon the line of attack. The ankle may be either bent (toes pointing sideways) or extended (toes pointing down). In some styles, a bent ankle is often used to hook the leg upward during a deflecting block. Common variations are:

48. Inside Leg Block
Raise the lead leg and turn the knee inward, covering the groin. The knee points about 45° forward. This block can quickly shift into a Stamp Kick or Side Kick counter.

49. Outside Leg Block
Raise the lead leg and turn the knee outward about 30°. The lower leg angles inward to protect the groin against rising kicks. This block is usually used against circular kicks. Outside Leg Blocks against straight kicks are risky, since you expose your groin. This block can quickly shift into a Front Kick, Reverse Roundhouse Kick or Circular Inner-Heel Kick.

50. Rear Leg Block
Raise the rear leg, with the knee pointing about 30° forward. This block is usually used against circular kicks, such as a Roundhouse or Spin Kick; and can quickly shift into a Front Kick, Crescent Kick, or Roundhouse Kick.

Hand strikes are an important form of attack and defense found in a great many martial arts. They are also quite likely the most common form of attack encountered during self-defense and combat. Consequently, it is not only important to master the hand strikes themselves, but also common defenses against them. Most comprehensive martial arts incorporating strikes, also contain defenses against them. Although this chapter is titled "Defense Against Punches," these counters can be used against almost any form of hand

DEFENSE AGAINST PUNCHES

strike, since the crucial factor is the strike's direction, not the formation of one's hand. The following pages will provide an overview of defensive principles, followed by typical counterstrikes used in Hapkido, which are also found in other martial arts. The examples shown are meant to be used as a starting point. Once you grasp basic concepts and methods of application, try to develop a more intuitive method of countering, based on the flow of combat, not your desire to use a specific technique. Many possibilities exist.

BASIC CONCEPTS

In eclectic martial arts like Hapkido, strikes are countered using a blend of counterstrikes, holds, and throws. Technique selection and sequence is up to the user. Regardless of how you attempt to counter a strike, you must first commit one of the following actions:

• Block and counterstrike
• Block and apply a hold
• Block and apply a throw
  (*block* means to block or avoid)

Any of these three initial responses can be followed by more strikes, holds, or throws, in any order you wish, as circumstances dictate. Of these three methods, *counterstriking* will be discussed in this text, since this is a book about striking, and counterstriking is also one of the most important and basic forms of defense. Defenses using holds or throws are covered in the author's companion books: *The Art of Holding*, *The Art of Throwing*, and *Hapkido: Traditions, Philosophy, Technique*.

Counterstriking

When defending against strikes, three basic methods of counterstriking are used:

• Block first, then strike
• Block and strike simultaneously
• Avoid and strike simultaneously

In all three methods, blocks are combined with avoiding movements, such as stepping or slipping. These three basic methods are shown on the opposite page, using typical hand strikes. The same principles are also applied when using kicks, or blocking and striking against kicks.

1. Block First, Then Strike

This is the simplest form of counterattack, and the first method to be learned by novices. Blocking and striking should be executed in quick succession, in a manner often referred to as "touch and go." If you move too slowly, the opponent will avoid your strike. You may use one hand to block and the other to strike, or use the same hand for both actions.

2. Block and Strike Simultaneously

In this form of counterattack, execution speed is increased by combining two separate movements into one—a basic principle in Hapkido. Your counterstrike lands before the opponent's blow can be retracted. This requires excellent timing and anticipation. The faster your opponent, the more difficult this becomes. In these situations, use feints to draw a specific attack, so you are not depending entirely on reflexes or guesswork. Against a quicker opponent, feinting will help negate their superior speed by allowing you to react sooner. When compared to the previous method, (*block first, then strike*), blocking and striking simultaneously is often more effective, since you are striking while your opponent is still committed to their strike. It can also be safer, since you are hitting in the brief moment between their blows. Remember, most opponents will be executing strikes in rapid combinations, not slow single blows or stepping lunge punches. This is true even of unskilled street-fighters.

Basic Methods of Defense (against strikes)

Block and Counterstrike

Block and Hold

Block and Throw

3. Avoid and Strike Simultaneously

In this form of counterattack, you will move to avoid the blow (without blocking), as you simultaneously deliver a counterstrike. *Avoiding* the blow is accomplished by stepping (when time permits), or by moving your body without stepping. Basic avoiding movements were discussed previously in the *Avoiding + Blocking* chapter (slip, duck, step away, etc.). When avoiding and striking simultaneously, subsequent strikes can be delivered more quickly, since the second hand (or foot) is not concerned with blocking. Thus, it is ideally positioned to follow behind the first counterstrike, before an opponent adjusts or moves out of range. This is the most sophisticated form of counterattack, requiring superb reflexes and timing. If your timing is off you may be struck. However, against a fast, highly skilled opponent, it may provide your only opportunity to land a blow. If you find yourself flailing at empty space, this is a good clue. Feints and evasive movement are usually important in these types of counters.

Methods of Counterstriking

Block First, Then Strike

Block and Strike Simultaneously

Avoid and Strike Simultaneously

Technical Concerns

The basic blocks and strikes outlined in earlier chapters can be combined in limitless ways when counterattacking. The following pages show a range of possibilities; many others exist. Although these counters are typically called *Defense Against Punches,* they can be applied against any form of hand strike, a push, or an attempt to grab. The direction of an opponent's attack is usually the crucial factor. The most common strike deliveries are straight, inside circular (hooking), and outside circular (backhand motion). Rising and descending attacks are less common. If you do not understand the mechanics of individual blocks and strikes, refer to previous chapters. The sequences shown on the following pages should be executed very quickly, and practiced from both sides (changing leads). Blocks or strikes to pressure points are based on medical principles covered in *Hapkido: Traditions, Philosophy, Technique* (same author).

Refining Technique

When blocking and counterstriking, try to create combinations that are biomechanically efficient. The body movements used to block will suggest subsequent movements that can be used in striking. The most effective combinations are usually *very fast* and *very simple.* Anything you can do to reduce the time between your block and counterstrike will increase your chances of success. Long, traditional arm movements with excessive footwork look very pretty in demonstrations; however, they are usually far too slow to be effective in real combat.

Modernizing Technique

Most of the techniques in this chapter have roots in older, traditional techniques, but have been modernized by the author to reflect contemporary trends in self-defense and combat. Specifically, most techniques are shown *without* the pronounced footwork, rooted stances, and long deliveries often seen in traditionally oriented schools. Traditional motions were discussed in earlier chapters covering basic strikes and blocks.

1. Against Straight Punch

B. L Inside Parry (or Inside Block)
C. R Straight Punch to cheek
D. L Narrow Hook Punch to jaw

Step or slip outside, as you block and strike (very fast combo). Hit the cheek at ST-2, and the jaw at ST-4 or ST-5. Turn your shoulders and hips as you punch. Make sure your shoulder-turn launches the punch, not the opposite. Keep your head behind your shoulder for safety.

2. Against Straight Punch

B. L Inside Block
C. R Inside Elbow Strike
D. L Inside Elbow Strike

Step or slip outside, as you block and strike. Execute at close range, or by stepping sideways and forward, toward opponent. Block the elbow at TW-11. Strike the ribs at LV-13, or both GB-24 and LV-14. The next blow strikes the kidney at GB-25, or the back of the head at GB-20.

3. *Against Straight Punch*

B. L Downward Semicircular Parry
C. R Inside Elbow Strike
D. L Uppercut Punch

Use against a charging attacker, or step forward to attacker's outside as they strike. Step, parry, and trap the arm, as you pivot your entire body into the elbow strike (rotate your shoulders). Pivot to your right and deliver an Uppercut Punch to the ribs at SP-21, or kidney at GB-25.

4. *Against Straight Punch*

B. L Inside Parry
C. R Straight Punch
D. R Side Kick

Slip inside as you parry and strike. Exercise caution when moving to the inside, since you are vulnerable to a rear-hand strike. Be ready to parry at any time, usually with your lead hand. Strike the face, jaw, or temple. Kick the inner knee at SP-9, SP-10, or LV-8 to topple attacker.

5. *Against Straight Punch*

B. L Outside Parry
C. R Overhead Punch
D. R Shin Kick or
    Circular Inner-Heel Kick

Slip outside as you parry and strike. You can also use a rear straight punch, if attacker drops their lead. In either case, your punch crosses over their jab. Try to punch before they retract their fist. Keep your left hand up, guarding against a rear punch.

6. *Against Straight Punch*

B. L Outside Grab Parry
C. R Inside Hammer Fist Strike
D. R Inside Hook Kick

Slip outside as you parry and strike. Try to grab the wrist or clothing. Pull opponent's arm across their body to expose their ribs and cut off a rear-hand punch. If you can't grab, *stick* to the arm and push it into their face. Strike the ribs or kidney at GB-25 (B). Kick to the outer thigh at GB-31, or the side or back of the knee.

7. *Against Straight Punch*

B. R Inside Parry and
   L High Straight Punch
C. R Uppercut Punch
D. Roundhouse Kick

Slip outside as you parry and strike simultaneously. You can also strike using a Hook Punch; or a Ridge Hand to the throat, hitting both ST-9 and ST-10. Follow with a straight Uppercut Punch to the ribs at SP-21. Kick the ankle to your left, to topple attacker.

8. *Against Straight Punch*

B. L Outside Parry and
   R Knuckle Hand Strike
C. L Overhead Punch
D Front Heel Kick

Step inside or pivot, as you parry and strike. Watch out for a rear-hand punch. The first strike is high to the throat at CO-23, with your chin tucked behind your shoulder (low blows expose your head). Hit the solar plexus at CO-15, or belly, raking CO-3, 4, 5, and 6. As the head comes forward, kick up to the underside of the chin.

171

9. Against Straight or Hook

B. L Outside Knife Hand Block
   R Inside Knife Hand Strike
C. L Inside Knife Hand Strike
D. L Rising Knee Strike (pull head)

Step inside or pivot your body, as you block and strike simultaneously. Block the wrist at LI-5. Strike both sides of the neck at LI-18. Without withdrawing your hands, pull the head downward into the knee strike. The acupoints struck are related.

10. Against Straight or Hook

B. Combined or Two-Hand Grab Parry
C. R Outside Knife Hand Strike
D. R Inside Elbow Strike

Step inside or pivot your body as you parry with both hands. Grab the wrist or clothing, striking as you pull opponent into each blow. Strike with your Knife Hand to the temple or neck (Back Fist also works well). Collapse your elbow and thrust it inward to your left, hitting the face or jaw.

11 A

12 A

11. Against Uppercut Punch

B.   L Pressing Forearm Block
C.   R Rising Elbow Strike
D.   R Rising Knee Strike

From close range, trap opponent's arm early in its delivery, and strike the chin. Keep your opposite hand up, guarding against a rear strike (B). The Rising Elbow Strike to the underside of the chin also protects your head. Pull the head down. Drive your knee upward into the groin or head.

B

B

12. Against Uppercut Punch

B.   L Ox Jaw Block
C.   R Hook Palm Heel Strike
D.   R Shin Roundhouse Kick

Block firmly to the inner elbow at PC-3, or mid-inner forearm (nerves), or PC-6 (above inner wrist). Strike either the nose, temple at TW-23, or jaw at TW-17, ST-4, or ST-7. You can also strike using an Inside Elbow Strike. Kick the thigh at GB-31, using your shin or instep (based on range).

C

C

D

D

13. Against Straight Punch

B.   R Semicircular Parry
C.   L Straight Back Hand Strike
D.   R Straight Palm Heel Strike

Redirect a lead jab downward, as you shuffle inward, striking pressure points on the face or side of the head (e.g., GV-26, ST-3, ST-5, ST-7). This is a very fast combination that can be used to set up close range strikes with the elbows, forearms, or knees, or to enter holds or throws.

14. Against Hook Punch

B.   R Reverse Outside Block
C.   R Hook Palm Heel Strike
D.   R Inside Elbow Strike

Step forward or back into a short Back Stance, as you block outward. As you stop the blow, hook your Palm Heel inward (pivot your front foot), striking the side of the nose, or back of the jaw (TW-17). Continue your inward motion, also striking the head with your elbow. Option: skip C.

15. *Against Straight Punch*

B. L Inside Parry, R Open Hand Strike
C. L Inside Elbow Strike, arm lock
D. R Outer Forearm Strike

Charge forward to the outside as you parry a lead strike. At the same time, hit upward to the testicles with your Open Hand. Swing your L elbow over opponent's shoulder and into their head, as you trap their wrist and lock their elbow on your chest. Swing your forearm into the upper lip at GV-26.

16. *Against Straight or Hook*

B. Two-Hand Grab Parry
C. L Inside Elbow Strike
D. L Outside Elbow Strike, Stamp Kick

Step inside and grab opponent's arm with both hands. Continue to turn as you lift your elbow, striking the jaw or chin. Retract your elbow and hit opponent's head from the opposite direction, pulling them into your blow. Stomp on their foot at the same time. Repeat elbow strikes as needed.

17. *Against Lead Hook Punch*

B. R Head Block
C. Weave, L Straight Punch
D. Weave, R Uppercut Punch

Against a blow you can't avoid, use a shield block (B), then weave outside to punch the ribs from a safer position. Weave back inside and snap an uppercut punch to the chin. Weaving is used to make targeting difficult for your opponent, as you execute counterstrikes.

18. *Against Straight or Uppercut*

B. Face Block (with both arms)
C. R Straight Punch
D. Weave, L Straight or Hook Punch

Against a blow you can't avoid, use a shield block (B). As you detect a pause, thrust your fist or fingers into the eye or cheek. Weave or step outside to strike the ribs or groin, using a Hook Punch or Straight Punch (depending on distance). Weaving is crucial to evade other blows.

19. *Against High Punch*

B. High X Block
C. R Back Elbow Strike
D. R Descending Back Fist Strike

Against straight or descending blows, execute an X Block as you step forward. Grab the wrist, pivot 180° without stepping, thrusting your body into opponent as you strike the solar plexus at CO-15, then the bridge of the nose at M-HN-4, or lower forehead at M-HN-3. This should be a fast combo.

20. *Against Twin C Punch*

B. Scissor Block
C. L Descending Back Fist Strike
D. R Front Kick (fade-away)

After blocking, your lower hand follows a vertical circular path to strike the bridge of the nose at M-HN-4. Kick the groin or belly using your rear leg. If you are too close, fade-away by using a fast draw-step or jump, to set up the kick. Do not take a full step, since it is too slow.

1. Against Left-Right Combo

B. R Inside Parry
C. L Rising Block and R Shin Kick
D. L Front Thrust Kick (with heel)

Step inward as you execute two blocks and a Shin Kick, in one fluid motion. The two blocks deflect a left-right combination. If opponent steps back, execute a Front Thrust Kick to the belly (D). If they are close, execute a R Rising Elbow Strike, or a R Inside Elbow Strike.

2. Against Lead Straight Punch

B. L Outside Parry
C. R Roundhouse Kick
D. L Spin Kick

Slip or step outside as you execute a Roundhouse Kick to the back of the knee. If you are confident of your block, skip the slip or step, so the kick hits faster. If opponent steps back (D), deliver a Spin Kick to the temple, jaw, throat, or ribs. If they keep a L lead, kick the lower rear-skull or spine.

3. Against Lead Hook Punch

B. L Reverse Outside Block
C. L Side Thrust Kick
D. R Turning Back Kick

As you block, drive opponent backward with a thrusting kick to their ribs or lead hip. This exposes their targets for the next kick. Turn and kick without looking (faster). If opponent steps backward to avoid your Side Kick (stance changes), they will open targets for your second kick.

4. Against Lead Hook Punch

B. L Outside Knife Hand Block
C. L Side Snap Kick
D. R Side Thrust Kick

As you block, commence a fast Side Snap Kick to the lower leg or ankle, setting your foot quickly down (could be a Stamp Kick). As opponent withdraws their R leg (changing leads), deliver a Side Thrust Kick to the inner knee of the opposite leg. The first kick sets up the second (fast combination).

5. *Against Lead Straight Punch*

B. L Outside Grab Parry
    L Front Blade Kick (or Toe Kick)
C. R Front Heel Kick
D. R Side Thrust Kick

Step back into a short Back Stance or a Cat Stance, as you parry and kick simultaneously. Grab the arm and kick to the groin (lowers opponent's head). Follow with a heel kick to the underside of the chin. Without planting your foot, deliver a Side Kick to the knee.

6. *Against Lead Straight Punch*

B. R Outside Grab Parry
C. R Roundhouse Kick (Ball Foot)
D. L Inside Axe Kick (Back Heel)

Shift your weight to your rear leg, as you parry and grab (B). Pull opponent off-balance as you kick the testicles, or groin at LV-12 and SP-12. This bends them over for an Axe Kick to the spine at GV-14 or GV-11. If they don't bend, deliver a L Inside Hook Kick to the back of the knee or spine.

7 A

8 A

7. *Against Lead Straight Punch*

B. L Outside Grab Parry
C. R Inside Crescent Kick
D. R Low Side Kick

Slip or step outside as you parry and grab the arm. Pull it downward and across as you kick the side of the head. Without putting your leg down, kick the side or back of the knee. Do not kick high if you fail to control the arm (C), since you are vulnerable to a throw; instead go directly to D.

8. *Against Lead Straight Punch*

B. R Outside Grab Parry
C. R Outside Crescent Kick
D. R Roundhouse Kick (Ball Foot)

Turn your hips outward as you parry. Pull the arm down across opponent's body to expose the head and unbalance them. Kick the side of the head (C). Without planting your foot, kick to the groin (Ball Foot) or face (Instep). Do not kick high if you fail to control the arm (C), or you may be thrown.

B

B

C

C

D

D

1. Against Lead Punch

A. Attacker throws a straight or hook strike
B. Slip outside to avoid, R Straight Punch
C. L Straight Punch

As attacker throws a lead punch, slip outside with a R straight punch to the ribs. Immediately cross over their lead, with a R straight punch to the face, jaw, or temple. Execute very quickly without stepping, similar to the previous technique. Adding steps will slow delivery.

2. Against Rear Punch

A. Lean back to avoid
B. Snap forward, L Uppercut Punch
C. R Rising Elbow Strike

As attacker throws a rear punch, lean back and snap forward, punching to the abdomen or solar plexus. Use your rear hand to parry if needed. Follow with a Rising Elbow Strike to the underside of the chin; if you are too far away, use a Straight Punch or Uppercut Punch.

3. Against Rear Punch

A. Attacker throws a straight strike
B. Turn away to avoid
C. Snap forward, R Palm Heel Strike

As attacker throws a rear punch, turn away. If you misjudge the punch, use your lead shoulder or rear hand to parry. As the punch is fully extended, quickly snap forward, striking the head with any straight strike. Keep your chin tucked behind your shoulder to hinder a L hook.

4 A

B

C

5 A

B

C

6 A

B

C

4. *Against Straight Punch*

A. Attacker throws a straight punch
B. R Front Kick (with lead leg)
C. L Low Side Kick

As attacker punches, use a Front Kick to stop their forward movement. Slide your rear foot toward your front foot to launch the kick. Strike the abdomen, hip, groin, or outer thigh. Quickly retract your foot and plant it, to prevent being thrown. Follow with a Side Kick to either knee.

5. *Against Straight Punch*

A. Attacker throws a straight punch
B. Side Kick (with lead leg)
C. Hook Kick or Spin Kick (with rear leg)

As attacker punches, use a Side Kick to their lower leg, to stop their forward motion. You may also strike their hips to unbalance them. Slide your rear foot toward your front foot to launch the kick. Quickly plant your foot (to prevent a throw), spin 270°, and kick the back of the knee.

6. *Against Straight Punch*

A. Attacker throws a straight punch
B. L Turning Back Kick
C. R Back Side Kick

As attacker punches, turn and launch two kicks. Don't hesitate. Execute as soon as you detect motion. Kicking from a Side Stance is fastest, since you are already partially turned. Initially, your lead foot shifts slightly to the side, to set up the first kick. This combo is very practical.

Kicks are an important form of attack and defense found in a great many martial arts. Because these techniques can be very powerful, and devastating if they connect, any kicker must be considered a serious threat. Consequently, it is not only important to master the kicks themselves, but also common defenses against them. Most comprehensive martial arts incorporating kicks also contain defenses against them. The following pages will provide an overview of defensive principles, followed by typical counterstrikes used in

DEFENSE AGAINST KICKS

Hapkido, which are also found in other martial arts. The examples shown are meant to be used as a starting point. Once you grasp basic concepts and methods of application, try to develop a more intuitive method of countering, based on the flow of combat, not your desire to use a particular technique. Be aware that there are literally thousands of possible responses to any given situation. Many of the strikes covered in the "Combinations" chapter can also be used to defend against kicks, if preceded by a block or avoiding movement.

BASIC CONCEPTS

In eclectic martial arts like Hapkido, kicks are countered using a blend of counterstrikes, holds, and throws. Technique selection and sequence is up to the user. Regardless of how you attempt to counter a kick, you must first commit one of the following actions:

- Block and counterstrike
- Block and hold
- Block and throw
  (*block* means to block or avoid)

Any of these initial responses can be followed by additional strikes, holds, or throws, in any order you wish, as circumstances dictate. Of these three methods, *counterstriking* will be covered in this text, since this is a book about striking, and counterstriking is also one of the most important and basic forms of defense. When defending against kicks, throwing techniques can also be highly effective. Defenses using holds or throws are covered in the author's companion books: *The Art of Holding*, *The Art of Throwing*, and *Hapkido: Traditions, Philosophy, Technique.*

Counterstriking

Counterstrikes can be used to discourage further attack, knock an opponent to the ground, or set up a throw. The three methods of counterstriking, described in the *Defense Against Punches* chapter, are also used when defending against kicks. They are:

- Block first, then strike
- Block and strike simultaneously
- Avoid and strike simultaneously

In all three methods, blocks are combined with avoiding movements, such as stepping or slipping. These three basic methods are shown on the opposite page, using typical leg strikes. The same principles are also applied when using hand strikes. Generally, you can avoid many kicks by stepping closer (too close to kick), or stepping further away (out of range). Generally, the most critical factors in countering kicks are timing the counter and using proper footwork to optimize technique.

Timing the Counter

From the moment the kicking leg is raised until it is set back down, the kicker is vulnerable. Their balance is compromised and their mobility is limited as long as one leg is suspended. Once the kick is launched, an attacker is essentially committed to this action until the kick is completed and the foot is returned to the ground. Whether you are counterstriking, holding, or throwing, this brief span of time is the key moment when a counter must be launched to be successful.

Consequently, timing is crucial. If you move too soon, your opponent will redirect the kick. If you move too late, the opponent will adjust to your counter, or hit you with a second technique before you can apply your counter. Against an excellent kicker, the *moment of vulnerability* becomes much briefer, since the kicker's transitions between techniques will occur more rapidly. When your counters fail, it is usually because you have missed the moment. Use feints and evasive movements to negate the speed of a faster opponent.

Basic Methods of Defense (against kicks)

Block and Counterstrike

Block and Hold

Block and Throw

Avoiding Footwork

Footwork is very important in positioning your body, to optimize a technique or avoid the blow. Many techniques in this chapter can be executed from a variety of stances using a variety of different steps. Don't become overly concerned with using "correct footwork." The dynamics of combat do not allow for such a rigid approach. Learn to execute techniques from a variety of positions, awkward or otherwise. Regardless of how you step, the direction of your movement is usually determined by the type of strike you are countering, with the following generally true. Against straight kicks, such as a Front Kick, Side Kick, or Back Kick: step in at an angle, side step, or back away. Against circular strikes, such as a Roundhouse or Spin Kick: duck, back away, or step inside the kick at a 45° angle *away* from the strike. When in doubt, or if you're overwhelmed, turn and launch a Back Kick. This protects your head and is very difficult to defend against. If you learn nothing else, learn to apply a Back Kick.

Methods of Counterstriking

Block First, Then Strike

Block and Strike Simultaneously

Avoid and Strike Simultaneously

Technical Concerns

The basic blocks and strikes outlined in earlier chapters can be combined in limitless ways when counterattacking against kicks. The following pages show typical counter-strike combinations against major types of kicks. Many other possibilities exist, some of which are shown in the author's 1136-page book on Hapkido. Many of the kick combinations listed in the *Combinations* chapter can also be adapted for defense against kicks. In defensive applications, you will merely set up the combination by using a block or avoiding movement first. Remember, counterstriking is essential an offensive action initiated after an opponent's offensive action. Consequently, virtually any response is possible given an appropriate situation.

When learning and applying kick defenses, it is important to realize that many defenses used against a particular kick can often be employed against numerous other kicks. The crucial factor is the direction of an opponent's attack. The most common kick deliveries are straight (thrusting front kicks, side kicks, back kicks), rising circular (front kicks), inside circular (roundhouse kicks), and outside circular (hook kicks, spin kicks). Descending kicks are less common. If you do not understand the mechanics of individual blocks and strikes, refer to the earlier chapters covering this material. The sequences shown on the following pages should be executed very quickly, and practiced from both sides (changing leads).

Refining Technique

When blocking and counterstriking, try to create combinations that are biomechanically efficient. The body movements used to block will suggest subsequent movements that can be used in striking. The most effective combinations are usually *very fast* and *very simple*. Anything you can do to reduce the time between your block and counterstrike will increase your chances of success. When counterkicking in self-defense situations, low kicks are usually preferred; however, high kicks can also work well if used appropriately.

1. Against Front Kick

B.   R Raking Back Fist Block
C.   R Back Fist Strike
D.   L Straight Punch

Step inside to avoid the kick. Rake the surface of the leg, striking several pressure points (e.g., GB-37, 38, 39). The block is actually more of a *strike* than a block. Follow with a Back Fist to the temple (M-HN-9 or TW-23), and a Straight Punch to the jaw (ST-4) or ribs (LV-14).

2. Against Front, Side or Round

B.   Back step to avoid kick
C.   R Descending Elbow Block
D.   R Spear Hand

With or without stepping, drop your lead elbow into the kick's trajectory, allowing the foot to hit into the point of your elbow. As attacker plants their foot (moving forward), thrust a Spear Hand into their eyes, as you slide your front foot forward for power and to increase your reach.

3. *Against Front Kick*

B. L Inside Low Block (lead hand)
C. R Straight Punch
D. L Hook Punch

Take a short step outside, as you block. Pivot your body when stepping, in case your block fails. As attacker plants their foot, deliver a Straight Punch to their temple or face, and a Hook Punch to their kidney (GB-25) or ribs (SP-21). Turn the hips and shoulders for power.

4. *Against Front Kick*

B. L Descending Palm Heel Block
C. R Roundhouse Kick
D. L Descending Knife Hand Strike

Step back as you block to the instep. As opponent plants their foot, kick to the groin (SP-12 and LV-12) or testicles. As they bend over, push the head down (or pull hair) and strike down to the base of the skull at GB-20, BL-10, or GV-15. Option: use a L Descending or Inside Elbow Strike for step D.

5. Against Side Thrust Kick

B. L Inside Hook Block (lift leg)
C. R Inside Elbow Strike
D. R Back Fist Strike

Step 45° forward to the outside as you block and lift. Hit down to the knee, or the nerve along the thigh (GB-30, 31, or 32). Follow with a Back Fist to the back of the head (GB-20), or side of the jaw (TW-17). If the head is too far, hit the kidney (GB-25) or execute a R Side Kick.

6. Against Side Kick

B. Side step, R Outside Scoop Block
C. R Low Side Kick
D. Pin knee with blade of foot

Steps outside with your lead foot as you parry and scoop the leg. Pull up to unbalance, as you kick the back of the knee. Keep thrusting forward and down, driving their kneecap into the ground. Pin the knee as you lift and wrap the other leg. Lock the ankle: press your wrist into the Achilles tendon, keep the instep extended.

7. *Against Side Kick*

B. Draw step, R Outside Scoop Block
C. L Low Side Kick
D. Lift leg, throw backwards

The front draw step is essential to *quickly* avoid and set up your Side Kick. Draw your front foot toward your rear foot as you deflect and scoop the kick. Weight your R leg as you pivot and kick the knee. Lift the leg and step forward, unbalancing attacker backward to force a fall.

8. *Against Side Kick*

B. R Outside Scoop Block
C. R Rising Blade Kick
D. L Standing Low Spin Kick

Parry and scoop the leg, as you lean back and kick up to the inner knee. Plant your foot to initiate a turn step. Deliver a Spin Kick or Side Kick to the back of the knee to topple attacker. This should be a *very fast* combo. Both kicks hit, before attacker regains a stable stance. You can also use a Drop Spin Kick for D (more difficult).

9. Against Roundhouse Kick

B. L Outside Wrap Block
C. R Outer Forearm Strike
D. R Rising Knee Strike

Step inside. Block, wrap and lift the leg with one arm. The other arm hits the side of the head, then wraps behind the neck, or grips hair or clothing. Pull down at the head or shoulder, as you lift your knee into the solar plexus, ribs, chest, or face. High kicks require a Two-Hand Wrap Block.

10. Against Roundhouse Kick

B. Two-Hand Wrap Block
C. R Roundhouse Kick
D. R Low Side Kick (Knife Foot)

Step inside as the lead hand blocks and the rear hand wraps under the leg. Lift the leg to unbalance, as you kick the ribs at LV-13 (Instep Foot), or groin at LV-12 and SP-12 (Ball Foot). Without planting your foot, retract your leg and kick the inner knee at LV-8 or SP-10, toppling opponent.

11. *Against Roundhouse Kick*

B. Begin turn-step to avoid kick
C. R Turning Back Kick
D. L Roundhouse Kick

This counter is executed without blocking. As you detect the kick, quickly turn and deliver a Back Kick to attacker's open side, hitting the belly or chest. At close distances use an Uppercut Back Kick. Follow with a Roundhouse Kick to the back of the knee or calf, to topple attacker.

12. *Against Roundhouse Kick*

B. R Inside Leg Block
C. R Low Side Kick
D. R Outside Hammer Fist Strike

Lift your lead leg and block inward. Try to block to attacker's ankle or instep (more sensitive). Without putting your leg down, execute a Side Kick to the inner knee, followed by a Hammer Fist Strike to the temple or jaw. Your fist traces a horizontal circular path as you pivot.

13. Against Spin or Hook Kick

B. Two-Hand Wrap Block
C. R Rising Knee Strike
D. R Roundhouse Kick

Step forward, past attacker's heel. Your lead arm blocks as your rear arm wraps under the leg. Hold attacker's leg as you drive your knee up into their leg. Without putting your foot down, deliver a Roundhouse Kick to the left kneecap (support leg), groin, or head. You can also omit step C.

14. Against Spin or Hook Kick

B. Two-Hand Wrap Block
C. L Rising Knee Strike
D. L Low Side Kick

Step forward, past attacker's heel. Your lead arm blocks as your rear arm wraps under the leg. Drive your knee up into attacker's inner knee as you pull their leg down. Without planting your foot, kick the back of the knee, then pin it against the ground with your foot.

15. Against Outside Axe Kick

B. R Rising Block
C. L Hook Punch
D. R Descending Arch Kick

Step in close and block upward as the Axe Kick reaches its zenith. Pushing upward often causes a fall. Simultaneously, execute a Hook Punch to the kidney at GB-25. Follow with a Descending Arch Kick to the back of the knee, forcing a fall. Assist by pulling clothing or hair.

16. Against Knee Strike

B. L Inside Leg Block
C. L Stamp Kick, Side Head Butt
D. R Rising Knee Strike

This example shows how your legs can be used at close range, when your hands are occupied (e.g., grappling). Lift your leg to block a Roundhouse Knee Strike. As you plant your foot, stomp the toes or instep, and deliver a head butt to the nose. Lift your knee into the groin.

The defenses shown in this chapter are meant to show how strikes can be used

to free yourself from simple holds, such as wrist grabs, clothing grabs, chokes,

and holds from behind. There are also a great many other methods of defense

that are more commonly used in these situations, such as levering escapes,

joint locks, and throws. When using strikes to free yourself from a hold, it is

important to recognize that you are escalating force and your opponent will

likely respond in a similar manner. For this reason, strikes are usually not your

DEFENSE AGAINST HOLDS

first response, unless justified by circumstances. Strike defenses against simple

grabs and holds are most appropriate when your safety is seriously threatened

or you are facing multiple attackers. Strike counters are also very useful for

smaller people facing larger, overpowering opponents. In these situations,

joint locks and throws may start to fail, or you may be unable to begin the

initial movements needed to enter these techniques. This chapter presents

eight examples of strikes used against holds. Many other possibilities exist.

1. Against Double Grab to One Wrist

Attacker grabs your wrist with both hands. Form a Live-Hand (A). Push your hand forward, then pull it forcefully backward toward your waist, as you step forward and strike the jaw (ST-4 or ST-7), temple, or face with a downward Inside Elbow Strike (B). Continue the motion with a Shoulder Butt to attacker's chest, as you grip the edge of your clenched hand (C). Pull upward as you step backward and pivot 180°, levering your wrist free (D). Deliver an Outside Hammer Fist to the jaw or temple (E).

Important Points

This counter is characterized by three opposing circular movements that are linked, with each technique leading into the next. During the wrist escape portion, your 180° body-turn and backward momentum are essential for generating power (C–D), as your elbow traces a vertical circular path. This counter can also be applied without strikes, in which case it becomes a simple wrist escape.

2. Against Double Grab to One Wrist

Attacker grabs your wrist with both hands. Form a Live-Hand (A). Step forward between attacker's legs. Break the hold by grasping the edge of your open hand, and circling your elbow upward, forward, and downward between attacker's arms (B). Your elbow traces a vertical circular path with your wrist as a fulcrum. Continue pulling away high (C). Execute a Side Elbow Strike to the ribs or solar plexus (D), a Rising Knife Hand Strike to the groin (E), and a Back Fist Strike to the bridge of the nose at M-HN-3 or M-HN-4 (F).

Important Points

This is basically a simple wrist escape, with strikes added after the escape. When greater force is needed, execute a Shoulder Butt or Head Butt, as you initially step inward (B). After the Elbow Strike, immediately snap your Knife Hand into the groin, without retracting your elbow. Your strike traces a vertical circular path. The Descending Back Fist Strike to the nose can also be executed after step D.

Techniques 1 + 2:
When grasping your own hand to initiate the wrist escape portion of these techniques, your hand may be either closed (technique 1) or open (technique 2). Grab "open" when you will follow with open-hand strikes. Grasp your fist, when you will follow with closed-hand strikes.

3. Against Grab to Both Wrists

Attacker grabs both of your wrists. Form Live-Hands (A). Step backward and pull your hands toward your hips, forcing attacker to step forward or widen their stance (B). Circle your hands outward, up, and over. Grab both wrists and lock them by twisting them inward (C). Kick both knees outward at SP-10 or LV-8, to force a fall: deliver a R Roundhouse Kick to the lead inner-knee (D); without planting your foot, retract it, then deliver a R Side Kick to the rear inner-knee (E).

Important Points

When twisting and locking attacker's wrists, one hand is held vertical (push it toward attacker's armpit); the other is held horizontal (pull it toward your chest). Controlling the wrists helps to set up your kicks and control an opponent's movement; however, the locks are usually too weak to be finishing holds. The Roundhouse can be directed to the kneecap (use Ball Foot) or inner knee (use Instep Foot). The Side Kick uses a Knife Foot formation.

4. Against Grab to Both Wrists

Attacker grabs both of your wrists. Form Live-Hands (A). Drop your R foot back to stabilize your stance and pull your hands down. Circle both hands outward and over (B). Free both hands by driving your Knife Hands down into the wrists at SI-5 or SI-6. Push both hands to the side (C). Puncture both ear drums using two Open Hand Strikes, as you lift your knee into the groin (D). Without retracting your hands, pull attacker's head downward into a Rising Knee Strike to the face (E).

Important Points

When attacking the ear drums, swing both hands inward, along horizontal paths. Center your palms over the ear holes. Keep you palms stretched tight. This traps air and builds pressure in the ear chamber. Cupping your hands will not. Pull attacker's head down by wrapping your hands behind the skull, pulling both ears, or pulling hair. Many other strikes are possible (e.g., Twin Inside Palm Heel Strikes to both temples).

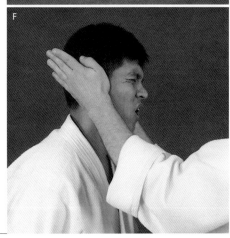

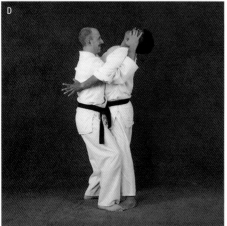

5. Against Front Bear-Hug

Attacker applies a bear-hug, pinning your arms (A). Lift your R foot, form Thumb Hands (B). Stomp attacker's instep or toes, gouge both thumbs into the hip joint at SP-12 (C), or ribs at GB-25. This loosens the bear-hug, creates maneuvering space, and frees your lower arms. Lower your body, reach around attacker's shoulders, and plant both of your Claw Hands on their face. Gouge your thumbs into nerves under the jaw, and your fingers into the eyes and cheek (ST-3). Push the head up, back, and down (D), forcing a fall (E).

Important Points

This counter can be used even if your lower arms are pinned. You must first create space, otherwise you will never be able to grip the head. The pressure points you are able to reach (C) depend upon: how tightly you are held, how much lower-arm movement is possible, and the relative sizes of your bodies. Any sensitive point you can reach will suffice. You can also pinch a small amount of skin at the front of the thigh; or at the side of the waist, just above the crest of the iliac bone.

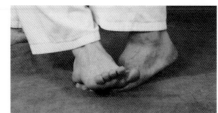

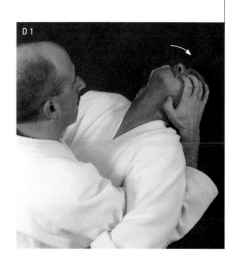

6. Against Rear Bear-Hug

Attacker applies a bear-hug, pinning your arms (A). Stomp one foot, then the other, using your heel or the edge of your shoe heel to strike the toes, or nerves between the metatarsal bones at GB-41 or LV-3 (B–C). Reach back and pinch the front of both thighs using Pincer Hands (D). When pinching, grab a small amount of skin, since it is more painful. Thrust both Spear Hands into the groin at SP-12 and LV-12 (E). As attacker backs away, drive them backward by executing a Back Kick to the groin or midsection (F).

Important Points

Other strikes can also be integrated into this counter. For example: hit the face with a Back Head Butt; kick back to the inner knee (SP-9, SP-10); kick down into the kneecap; or swing your heel back into the inner shin (KI-8, SP-6, LV-5), or upward to the testicles. While a single strike may not release the hold, several strikes have a cumulative effect. Vary strike locations to keep attacker guessing. Don't waste time repeating strikes that don't work; immediately switch to something else.

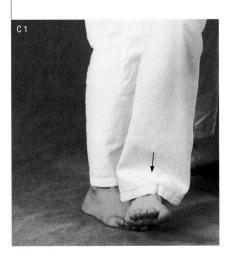

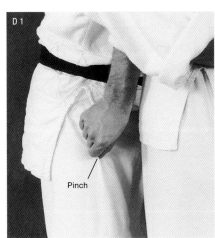

Pinch

SP-12 + LV-12

7. Against Front Naked Choke

Attacker applies a Front Naked Choke (A). Relieve pressure by pulling down on their arm with your L hand. The following strikes can be used singly or combined: Hook Punch (fist inverted) to the temple or back of the jaw (B), Spear Hand to the throat at CO-22 (C), Rising Thumb Fist to the testicles (D). As the choke loosens, drop your L hand down and pull the ankle, as you thrust your R Spear Hand into the groin at SP-12 and LV-12 (E), forcing a fall (F). Step C can also be used to force a fall.

Important Points

Front Naked Chokes are very dangerous holds. If an attacker can achieve proper lift and leverage, they will create extreme stress along the cervical spine and crush the windpipe. Always keep this in mind when selecting specific counters. This series of strikes targets different areas of the body, so if one fails another may connect. Execute rapidly, alternating or repeating strikes as needed. You can also pinch the inner thigh.

8. Against Two-Hand Choke

Attacker pulls you close and applies a Double Lapel Choke, with their arms crossed (A). Deliver a Twin Uppercut Punch to the ribs at LV-13 (B), then a Twin Hook Punch to both temples at M-HN-9 (C). Step back with your R foot, retract your R hand low and L hand high, shift your balance to your rear leg (D). Step forward and deliver a Twin C Punch, using Knuckle Hands to hit the throat at CO-23, and the groin at LV-12 and SP-12 (E). Drive attacker back as they release their hold.

Important Points
A skilled attacker will pull you in close to increase choke leverage. If they have proper grips, you can be choked unconscious very quickly. This counter uses a rapid series of devastating twin strikes to quickly break the choke. Modify your strike force based on the seriousness of the threat. Since you will hit the same pressure points on both sides of attacker's body, the effect is magnified. You can also hit both sides of the neck at LI-18.

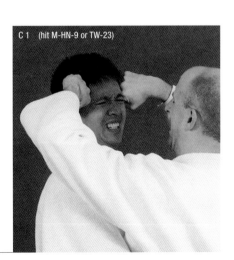

C 1   (hit M-HN-9 or TW-23)

E 1

FURTHER READING

Philosophy and Religion

Chan, Wing-Tsit, trans. and comp.
   A Source Book in Chinese Philosophy.
   Princeton NJ: Princeton University Press, 1963.

Earhart, Byron H, edit.
   Religious Traditions of the World.
   San Francisco: HarperCollins Publishers, 1993.

Smith, Huston.
   The Illustrated World's Religions:
   A Guide to Our Wisdom Traditions
   San Francisco: HarperCollins Publishers, 1994.

Zimmer, Heinrich.
   Philosophies of India.
   Edited by Joseph Campbell.
   Princeton NJ: Princeton University Press, 1969.

Medicine

Cohen, Kenneth S.
   The Way of Qigong: The Art and Science
   of Chinese Energy Healing.
   New York: Ballantine Books, 1997.

Dox, Ida; John Melloni; and Gilbert Eisner.
   The HarperCollins Illustrated Medical Dictionary.
   New York: HarperCollins Publishers, 1993.

Kaptchuk, Ted J.
   The Web That Has No Weaver:
   Understanding Chinese Medicine.
   New York: Congdon & Weed, 1983.

Maciocia, Giovanni.
   The Foundations of Chinese Medicine.
   London: Churchhill Livingston, 1989.

Netter, Frank H.
   Atlas of Human Anatomy.
   Summit, NJ: Novartis Pharmaceuticals, 1989.

Tedeschi, Marc.
   Essential Anatomy for Healing and Martial Arts.
   New York: Weatherhill, 2000.

Van Alphen, Jan, and Anthony Aris, editors.
   Oriental Medicine: An Illustrated Guide
   to the Asian Arts of Healing.
   Boston: Shambala Publications, 1997.

General Martial Arts

Draeger, Donn F., and Robert W. Smith.
   Comprehensive Asian Fighting Arts.
   New York: Kodansha, 1980.

Farkas, Emil, and John Corcoran.
   Martial Arts: Traditions, History, People.
   New York: Smith Publications, 1983.

Haines, Bruce A.
   Karate's History and Traditions.
   Tokyo: Tuttle, 1968.

Nelson, Randy F., edit.
   The Overlook Martial Arts Reader:
   Classic Writings on Philosophy and Technique.
   Woodstock NY: Overlook Press, 1989.

Tedeschi, Marc.
   The Art of Holding: Principles & Techniques.
   New York: Weatherhill, 2001.
   ———. *The Art of Throwing: Principles &*
   Techniques. New York: Weatherhill, 2001.
   ———. *The Art of Ground Fighting: Principles &*
   Techniques. New York: Weatherhill, 2002.

Periodicals

Aikido Journal. Tokyo, Japan.

Black Belt. Valencia, California.

Dragon Times. Thousand Oaks, California.

The Empty Vessel: A Journal of
   Contemporary Taoism. Eugene, Oregon.

Inside Karate. Burbank, California.

Inside Kung Fu. Burbank, California.

Internal Martial Arts. Collegeville, Pennsylvania.

Journal of Asian Martial Arts. Erie, Pennsylvania.

Taekwondo Times. Bettendorf, Iowa.

Tai Chi and Alternative Health.
   London, Great Britain.

Japanese Martial Arts

Draeger, Donn F.
   Classical Budo.
   New York: Weatherhill, 1996.

Funakoshi, Gichin.
   Karate-Do: My Way of Life.
   Tokyo: Kodansha, 1975.
   ———. *Karate-Do Kyohan: The Master Text.*
   Tokyo: Kodansha, 1973 (first published 1936).

Kano, Jigoro.
   Kodokan Judo.
   Tokyo: Kodansha, 1986 (first published 1956).

Kudo, Kazuzo.
   Dynamic Judo: Throwing Techniques.
   Tokyo: Japan Publications Trading Co., 1967.
   ———. *Dynamic Judo: Grappling Techniques.*
   Tokyo: Kodansha, c. 1967.

Nakayama, Masatoshi.
   Dynamic Karate.
   Tokyo: Kodansha, 1966.

Pranin, Stanley.
   Daito-ryu Aikijujutsu:
   Conversations with Daito-ryu Masters.
   New York: Aiki News, 1995.

Saotome, Mitsugi.
   The Principles of Aikido.
   Boston: Shambhala, 1989.

Ueshiba, Kisshomaru.
   Aikido.
   New York: Japan Publications, 1963.
   ———. *The Spirit of Aikido.*
   Tokyo: Kodansha, 1984.

Ueshiba, Morihei.
   Budo: Teachings of the Founder of Aikido.
   Tokyo: Kodansha, 1991 (first published 1938).

Chinese Martial Arts

Frantzis, Bruce Kumar.
The Power of Internal Martial Arts:
Combat Secrets of Ba Gua, Tai Chi, and Hsing-i.
Berkeley CA: North Atlantic Books, 1998.

Lee, Bruce.
Tao of Jeet Kune Do.
Santa Clarita, CA: Ohara Publications, 1975.

Yang, Jwing-Ming.
Taiji Chin Na: The Seizing Art of Taijiquan.
Boston MA: YMAA Publication Center, 1995.

Korean Martial Arts

Cho, Sihak H.
Korean Karate: Free Fighting Techniques.
Tokyo: Tuttle, 1968.

Chun, Richard, and P.H. Wilson.
Tae Kwon Do: The Korean Martial Art.
New York: Harper & Row, 1976.

Kimm, He-Young.
Hapkido 2.
Baton Rouge, LA: Andrew Jackson College
Press, 1994.
———. *Kuk Sool Korean Martial Arts.*
Baton Rouge, LA: Andrew Jackson College
Press, 1985.

Lee, Joo-Bang.
The Ancient Martial Art of Hwarangdo.
(three volumes)
Burbank CA: Ohara Publications, 1978.

Myung, Kwang-Sik, and Jong-Taek Kim.
Hapkido. (Korean language)
South Korea: 1967.

Suh, In Hyuk, and Jane Hallander.
The Fighting Weapons of Korean Martial Arts.
Burbank CA: Unique Publications, 1988.

Tedeschi, Marc.
Hapkido: Traditions, Philosophy, Technique.
New York: Weatherhill, 2000.

BOOKS BY MARC TEDESCHI

Hapkido: Traditions, Philosophy, Technique
Widely acclaimed the most comprehensive book
ever written on a single martial art, this text
contains over 2000 techniques encompassing
all forms of martial skills: strikes, holds, throws,
ground fighting, weapons, meditation, and
healing. Also included are in-depth chapters
on martial history, philosophy, and anatomy,
plus interviews with 13 renowned martial
artists. An authoritative presentation of basic
principles and techniques, integrated with
modern innovations, makes this work indispensible to martial artists of virtually any style.

1136 pages, 8 1/2 x 11 in.
Over 9000 b&w photos, maps, glossary, index
US $80.00 (hardcover), ISBN 0-8348-0444-1

Essential Anatomy For
Healing and Martial Arts
This book familiarizes healing practitioners
and martial artists with basic concepts of the
human body, as defined by both Western and
Eastern medical traditions. Written in a clear
and concise style, this text presents material
previously unavailable in any single text.
Also includes principles of pressure point
fighting, and 20 essential self-massage and
revival techniques, along with detailed tables
of acupoints in English, Chinese, Korean, and
Japanese, cross-referenced to nerves, blood
vessels, and other anatomical landmarks.

144 pages, 8 1/2 x 11 in., full-color
147 color drawings, 54 duotone photographs
US $19.95 (softcover), ISBN 0-8348-0443-3

Hapkido: An Introduction to
the Art of Self-Defense
The first introductory text to accurately portray
Hapkido in its entirety, this work is essential
reading for anyone seeking a concise, accurate
overview of Hapkido's history, philosophy, and
techniques. Contains basic material to guide
novices, plus more photographs and techniques
than any similarly priced competitive book.
The first edition also includes a coupon for
20% off the 1136-page *Hapkido* (see above).

128 pages, 8 1/2 x 11 in.
680 b&w photographs, 48 illustrations
US $16.95 (softcover), ISBN 0-8348-0483-2

The Art of Holding
This book outlines the core principles and
techniques that define the art of holding in
most martial arts. An in-depth presentation of
fundamentals is followed by over 155 practical
holds, including joint locks, chokes, nerve holds,
takedowns, pins, advanced combinations, and
defenses against joint locks and chokes.

208 pages, 8 1/2 x 11 in.
Over 1300 b&w photographs, 60 illustrations
US $29.95 (hardcover), ISBN 0-8348-0491-3

The Art of Throwing
This book outlines the core principles and
techniques that define the art of throwing in
most martial arts. An in-depth presentation of
fundamentals is followed by over 130 practical
throws, including shoulder throws, hip throws,
leg throws, hand throws, sacrifice throws,
combinations, and counterthrows.

208 pages, 8 1/2 x 11 in.
Over 1200 b&w photographs, 55 illustrations
US $29.95 (hardcover), ISBN 0-8348-0490-5

The Art of Ground Fighting
This book outlines the core principles and
techniques that define the art of ground fighting
in most martial arts. An in-depth presentation of
fundamentals is followed by over 195 practical
ground skills, including chokes, joint locks, pins,
ground kicks, sacrifice techniques, and counters
from seated, reclining, and kneeling positions.

208 pages, 8 1/2 x 11 in.
Over 1200 b&w photographs, 63 illustrations
US $29.95 (hardcover), ISBN 0-8348-0496-4

VIEW ONLINE
View samples or obtain information at:
www.tedeschi-media.com

HOW TO BUY
These books are available through retail
book stores or direct from the publisher:

Weatherhill, Inc.
41 Monroe Turnpike, Trumbull CT 06611 USA
Sales: 800-437-7840; 203-459-5090
Fax: 800-557-5601; 203-459-5095
order@weatherhill.com

The Art of
STRIKING

Designed and illustrated by Marc Tedeschi.

Principal photography by Shelley Firth and Frank Deras.

Creative consultation by Michele Wetherbee.

Editorial supervision by Ray Furse and Thomas Tedeschi.

Production consultation by Bill Rose.

The following individuals appeared with the author
in the photographs: Arnold Dungo and Cody Aguirre.

Also thanks to Merrill Jung for loaning
rare books from his personal collection.

The majority of the photographs were shot on
Plus-X Professional 2 ¼ film using Hasselblad cameras,
and were scanned from Ilford Multigrade prints
using an Epson ES-1200C flat-bed scanner.

Digital-type composition and page layout originated
on an Apple Macintosh 8500 computer.

Typeset in Helvetica Neue, Univers, Sabon,
Adobe Garamond, Weiss, and Times.

Printed and bound by Oceanic Graphic Printing
and C&C Offset Printing in China.

Published and distributed by Weatherhill.

Weatherhill

PUBLISHERS OF FINE BOOKS ON
ASIA AND THE PACIFIC